LOND
OXF

A long distance walk

PICCADILLY CIRCUS TO CARFAX TOWER

Richard James

Published by **Greatcities Publishing 2014**

ISBN: 978-0-9929347-1-2

With special thanks to all those who have helped me in the making of this book

FOLLOW THE COUNTRY CODE

- Keep to public footpaths on private land
- Close all gates
- Do not leave litter
- Keep dogs on a lead where appropriate, including on the downs and heaths during the bird nesting season
- Do not camp or light fires without the owners permission

Greatcities Publishing
gc10publishing@gmail.com

Printed by Dolman Scott Ltd
www.dolmanscott.co.uk

INTRODUCTION

This is a long distance walk from Piccadilly Circus in central London to Carfax Tower in the centre of Oxford, a distance of 93km. (60 miles approx). It is a walk of amazing varied scenery, from the striking historical buildings of London to the towpath of the Grand Union Canal, along the banks of the River Thames and finally to the dreaming spires of the University city of Oxford. At a steady pace, it can be completed typically in 6 days.

In addition to the Thames Path, the route takes us across the higher ground of the Chiltern Hills, to the west of Henley on Thames. This includes part of the Ridgeway path at Nuffield. Going this way is half the distance compared to that of following the River Thames past Reading. There are stations at convenient places, so that you may return to your base. (See also other information)

On a good, dry, sunny day this makes for a wonderful, enjoyable walk. Refreshments may be purchased along the way, or pack for a picnic, stopping at one of the many beauty spots. As well as just a walking experience, it is also designed to be fun, particularly with family members, or a group. Additional time spent exploring Marlow, Henley on Thames, Wallingford, Abingdon (if you follow the Thames Path) and Oxford is rewarding. Along the way you will get close to nature- magnificent trees, water birds, birds of prey, butterflies and a variety of flowers. Places of interest, quaint villages with their old churches and pubs, all add to the interest and variety of this remarkable walk.

CONTENTS

HISTORY

The buildings of this part of London mainly date from the Georgian and Victorian era, as London spread to the west from The Strand, Haymarket and fashionable St James. At Hyde Park Corner are found memorials to Wellington and the battle of Waterloo (1815), including the triumphal arch. The grand museums, legacies of the Great Exhibition of 1851, include the Victoria and Albert and the Natural History Museums. At Brentford, a monument records the crossing of the Thames by Caesar in 54B.C. and the battle that took place between Edmund Ironside and the Danish King Canute. The Grand Junction Canal, opened in 1814, enters into the Thames near Kew Bridge. At the height of canal building, 250,000 navvies-or inland navigators-were employed in their construction.

Much older relics from prehistoric times have been discovered in the countryside and in the Chiltern Hills. Ancient man and later those from the Bronze Age (around 1200 B.C.), left their mark. Old tracks, such as the Icknield Way and The Ridgeway were in use by the early travellers. Iron Age peoples from central Europe-the Celts and the Druids built settlements and hill forts in about 700 B.C.

Between 43 and 410 A.D., the Romans occupied the land. Their roads are encountered radiating from London. Dorchester-on-Thames became very important and alters to Jupiter and Augustus, coins and pavements have been unearthed. Its importance continued during Saxon times and after, when the missionary Birinus established a bishopric see and cathedral, of which nothing remains, although the Augustinian Abbey Church is still there for us to view.

Wallingford's old medieval bridge and the castle remains, destroyed after the Civil War, remind us of its past. Oxford, an important crossing place even before the 10th century, became a major seat of learning, particularly from the 13th century, when many great buildings and colleges were built, of which we are familiar with today.

WILDLIFE

Observing the wildlife, plants and trees can add to the enjoyment of our walk. Magnificent and stately trees are seen throughout, including the oak, beech and ash. There are several types of willow, as there are of poplar. One common type which is seen growing near the waterside, is the tall, columnar Lombardy poplar, introduced in 1758. Others are the sycamore, lime, hornbeam, young elm, alder, sweet (eating) chestnut - likely an introduction by the Romans and the horse chestnut. Many species of conifers are also noted, which include spruce, various types of pine and fir and the mighty Wellingtonia, or giant redwood.

Birds are seen on the water and by the riverside, in the trees and on the wing. They are also heard, such as the sharp 'chick' 'chick' call of the spotted woodpecker and the loud, laughing call of the green woodpecker. In the London area the ring-necked parakeet is seen and heard. These birds are an escapee and have spread to many parts. In addition to common garden birds, there are many types of water birds. Look out for coot, moorhen, grebe, various types of ducks, cormorant, redshank and swans. The bright blue coloured kingfisher is one of the most striking birds. Common birds of prey are the red kite and the buzzard, often seen on the wing in the countryside and over the hills.

The wild flowers are numerous in the spring and summer months. These include cranesbill (geranium), knapweed, toadflax, pennyroyal, thyme, lady's bedstraw, bellflower, vetch (of the pea family), white and red nettles, the blue flowered anchusa, rosebay willowherb, chicory, mallow, ragwort (yellow flowers), teasel and the dusky pink flowered hemp agrimony. In the water, note the white water lily (alba) and also the yellow flowered *nuphar lutea*. By the waterside the tall purple loosestrife, willowherb and Himalayan Balsam grow.

Butterflies seen in the spring and summer, may include the red admiral, peacock, painted lady, comma, fritillaries, meadow browns and those of the skipper family.

OTHER INFORMATION

The maps show the route we need to follow. They are set out simply and the scale varies as they cover a section-say from one village to the next. They should suffice but do not replace the excellent street atlases and maps produced by the O. S. Those maps are the 1.25 000 and the 1.50 000 scale which cover Reading and Windsor, the Chiltern Hills East, the Chiltern Hills West, Abingdon and Oxford.

There are various ways that you can do this walk from London to Oxford. You can plan your overnight stops, taking about 6 days to complete the route. Or, you may travel to and from a base in west London or from the Reading area. If you live further afield, it is possible to get to the starting point early on a Saturday by rail *off peak*. Use public transport or you car to get to and from the starting/finishing points. Stations are at Hammersmith, Chiswick, Kew Bridge, Iver, Cookham, Marlow, Henley and Oxford. A good bus service links Reading to Wallingford and Oxford. There is also a regular bus service from Didcot town centre to Wallingford. It may be convenient to do this walk over a long period, say at weekends when the weather is favourable, perhaps exploring places of interest, such as Marlow, Henley and Wallingford. On the first day you could cover Piccadilly to Kew Bridge section. On the second day, to Iver. On the third, to Cookham. Next, from Cookham to Henley, then from Henley to Wallingford and finally from Wallingford to Oxford, which is the longest section.

As far as possible busy road crossings are avoided, but some need to be crossed-such as the A412 Uxbridge Road. Always take care, especially if you are in a group or with children. Be vigilant and beware of cyclists along the riverside paths and the Thames Path at Oxford. The paths may be muddy after wet spells, such as during 2012. So dress accordingly. Sturdy, light, comfortable shoes are necessary.

If you wish to do this walk in reverse, starting from Oxford, always remember to reverse the right and left/ left and right directions and refer to maps.

MAP OF THE ROUTE

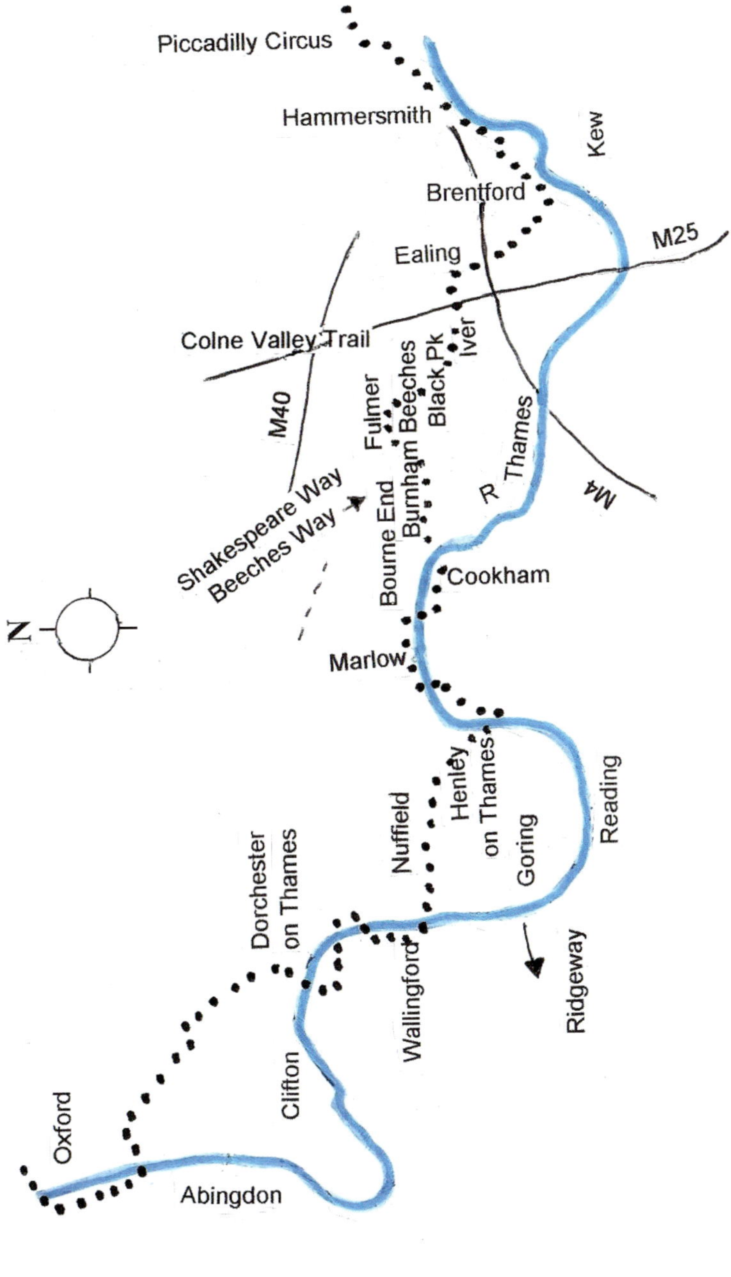

MAP

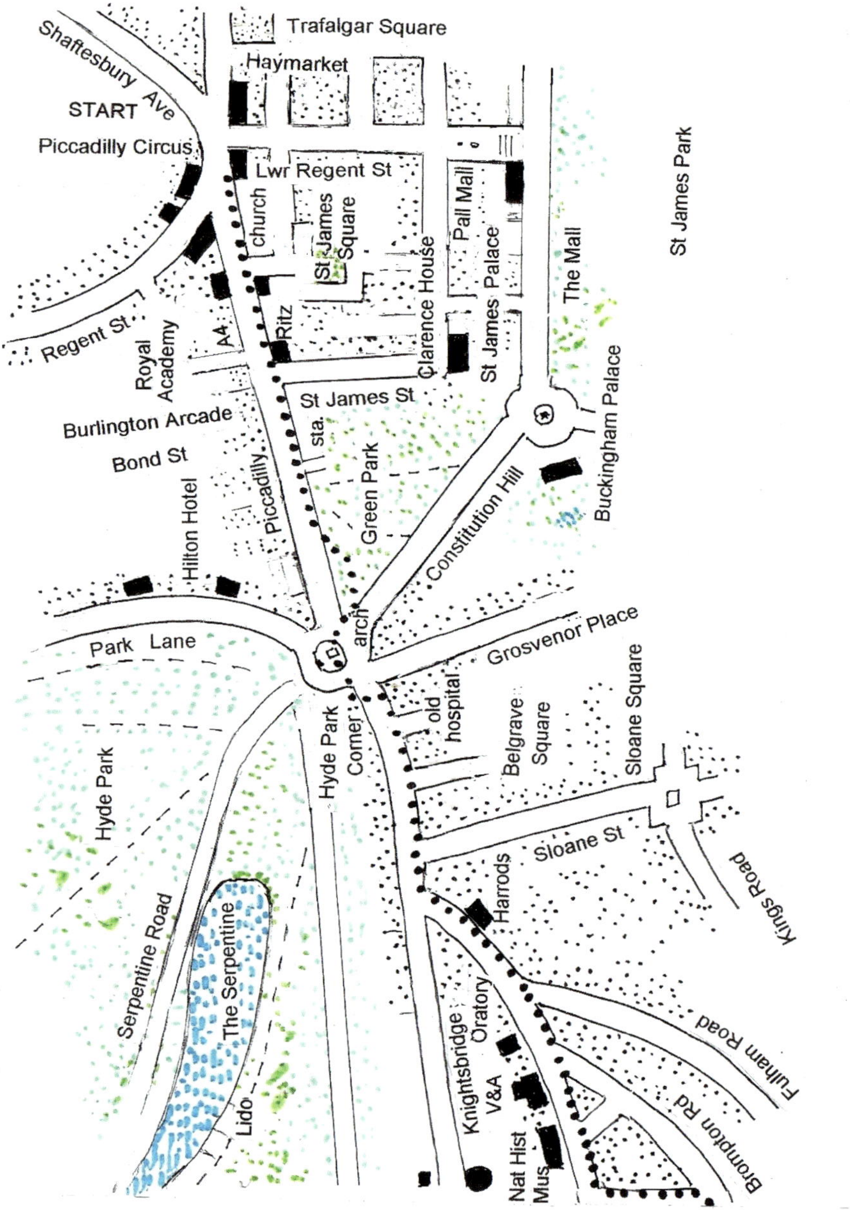
Trafalgar Square
Haymarket
Shaftesbury Ave
START
Piccadilly Circus
Lwr Regent St
church
St James Square
Pall Mall
St James Park
Clarence House
St James Palace
The Mall
Regent St
Royal Academy
A4
Ritz
St James St
Buckingham Palace
Burlington Arcade
Bond St
sta.
Piccadilly
Green Park
Constitution Hill
Hilton Hotel
arch
Park Lane
Grosvenor Place
old hospital
Belgrave Square
Sloane Square
Hyde Park
Hyde Park Corner
Sloane St
Kings Road
Harrods
Serpentine Road
The Serpentine
Oratory
Knightsbridge
V&A
Fulham Road
Brompton Rd
Lido
Nat Hist Mus

PICCADILLY CIRCUS TO KNIGHTSBRIDGE

Piccadilly Circus, Eros, Piccadilly and Regent Street, right

Known for its bright lights and figure of Eros, Piccadilly Circus lies between Trafalgar Square and Oxford Street in the West End of London. It was laid out in 1819 to coincide with the building of Regent Street at the junction with Piccadilly, between Regents Park and St James. The aluminium figure of "Eros" or "christian charity" commemorates Lord Shaftesbury, as does Shaftesbury Avenue to the east. The bright advertising lights have been here since 1910 and the colourful neon lights proliferated particularly in the 1920s.

Looking west we see the elegant Regency style curve of Regent Street (by John Nash). The broad way to the west is Piccadilly. Our walk begins here, so head this way. On the north side, opposite, is the Le Meridien Hotel and restaurant. The name Piccadilly comes from "Picadil", or "Piccadillies" the name of the high collar and is where these items were sold. They were very fashionable among the wealthy of St. James in the eighteenth century.

Next, on the left, we pass St. James' Church, designed by Wren and dating from 1684. It suffered some damage during the war. Famous for good food, Fortnum and Mason was founded in 1707. On the hour, when the clock strikes, the figures of Mr Fortnum and Mr Mason come out and bow to each other! Near the Piccadilly Arcade, opposite, notice Burlington Arcade, a famous covered walk with fine shops and security staff or "Beadles" on patrol.

St. James' Church, Piccadilly

Top: Burlington Arcade. Below: The Ritz Hotel

Ahead of us we pass under the arches of the famous Ritz Hotel (founded by the Swiss hotelier César Ritz in 1906). It is associated with luxurious service and afternoon teas. We walk past Green Park Station with views across London – the red brick tower of Westminster Cathedral being particularly noticeable in the distance. At the iron railings and the ornamental gates, go left into Green Park. This park is tree lined and devoid of flower beds and although the area was enclosed in the sixteenth century, it was soon after used as a burial ground for lepers. However it is popular with Londoners and visitors who congregate here in large numbers on sunny days. Buckingham Palace, the home of the Royal Sovereign, lies just beyond through the trees. A curving path, second right, swings around to exit the park where we find a memorial to those of the Indian sub-continent, who fell in the two world wars.

Green Park

The Wellington Memorial and arch, Hyde Park Corner

Opposite, on the traffic island is the Wellington Arch. Cross here, waiting for the lights to change at this very busy road. Once across, walk under the arch, passing the museum and notice Apsley House, right. This was the home of the Duke of Wellington (1769–1852) and in his day famously known as No1 London. The statue nearby, is of the Duke of Wellington seated upon his horse, Copenhagen.

Another monument is found here, The Royal Artillery Memorial, which is highly regarded for the quality of the bronze and stone figures. On the top, a great stone Howitzer gun points to the Somme, where these men lost their lives in 1915 –1918. The work, by Jagger, dates from 1925.

Hyde Park Corner

Buildings and Monuments

Apsley House

Gateway of Hyde Park

Duke of Wellington

Royal Artillery Memorial

Now cross this busy road again and turn left, then right. This leads us along the left side of Knightsbridge opposite Hyde Park. This park, along with Kensington Gardens, are the largest of the central London parks (Be aware of vehicles turning into these side roads). The road now bears left and soon we are approaching the magnificent façade of one of the world's most famous department stores - Harrods. In 1849, Henry Charles Harrod established a shop in Brompton Road. In 1905 the shop was moved to the larger premises that we know today in Knightsbridge.

Knightsbridge, Harrods and old London Routemaster bus

MAP

Nat Hist Mus
Queens
Gate
Old Brompton Road
Gloucester Rd
Kensington Road
supermarket
Collingham Rd
Road
Earls Court Rd
West Brompton Station
Brompton Cemetery
Chelsea F.C.
Cromwell
Warwick Rd
Earls Court
Empress State hotel
hotel
Peabody Est.
High Street
Cromwell Rd
Road
Lillie Road
Kensington
North End
West
St Andrews Ch
Star Rd
Greyhound Rd
Talgarth Rd
Charing Cross Hospital
Fulham Palace Road
school
Wilmslow Rd
Chancellors
River Thames
Hammersmith Road
Flyover
Hammersmith Bridge
Thames Path
Wetland Centre

KNIGHTSBRIDGE TO HAMMERSMITH

Walking past Harrod's

Continue to Brompton Oratory, which is noted for its musical tradition and its Baroque style. Dating from 1878-1884, it once the most important Catholic church in London and has a resemblance to St. Paul's cathedral. Next to it, as we proceed, more magnificent buildings come into view. The Victoria and Albert Museum in Cromwell Road features design, furniture, paintings and dress, it has seven miles of corridors! The foundation stone was laid by Queen Victoria in 1899 and the museum was finally opened by King Edward VII in 1909.

Brompton Oratory

Next to this is another grand and striking building; it is the very popular Natural History Museum which houses displays of animals, birds, the mighty blue whale and dinosaurs, as well as a large collection of meteorites. Back in 1851, proceeds from the Great Exhibition were used to purchase 80 acres of land for the erection of museums and other buildings to promote the sciences, music and art. This museum, with its pink and grey terracotta stone in Romanesque style, opened in 1881. Although some of the buildings were damaged during the second world war, these were re-built in 1960. Another popular museum here is the Science Museum.

The Victoria and Albert Museum

The Natural History Museum

Once we have passed these grand buildings, go left along Queens Gate; a fine terrace of houses. The church here, passed on our left is St. Augustine's (1876). It has a notable memorial to those fallen in the 1914-1918 war. It consists mostly of red brick, with other coloured brick and stone. At the end of Queens Gate turn right at the crossing and proceed into Old Brompton Road. The pub here is called The Duke of Clarence. London plane trees line the side of the road and are well suited to the city environment. There are shops at Bolton Gardens, and a clock stands out from the wall. Further, on the left, is the long wall of Brompton Cemetery, dated 1839 - West London and Westminster Cemetery. It covers about 40 acres and is the final resting place of some well known Londoners, including Sir Henry Cole, founder of the Victoria and Albert Museum, and Suffragette Emmiline Pankhurst.

Top: Queen's Gate ; St Augustine's church, Kensington.
Below: Along Old Brompton Road.

At the point where Old Brompton Road joins Lillie Road, is the Earls Court Exhibition Centre. Here the Boat Show and Royal Tournament have been staged. It was opened in 1887; the present building from 1937. Now the site awaits re-development. The Empress State building, roughly 300ft high, is about the same height of the giant ferris wheel which was constructed and opened here in 1895. The Earls Court underground station nearby, has the distinction of being the first in London to install an escalator, as long ago as 1911. The first section of the Piccadilly Line as far as Hammersmith, opened in 1906. The station here, however, is West Brompton.

We are now in Lillie Road and pass the Lillie Langtree pub and the Ibis Hotel. At block A of the Peabody Estate, go right into a footpath, then left past another hotel. We are now in North End Road. go right here, then at the Old Oak pub, go left along Star Road, passing St. Andrew's Church. Continue along Greyhound Road. An open space with graceful weeping willow trees is passed on our left.

The gateway of Brompton Cemetery.

**Earls Court and the Empress State Building.
Below: The Old Oak in North End Road**

St. Andrew's church, Star Road.
Below: The school, Fulham Palace Road.

Frank Banfield Park

Fulham Palace Road is the main road we now reach. Turn right, walking past the Southern Belle. Opposite, is a large school building dated 1901. At Charing Cross Hospital, Fulham, cross at the lights, go on and turn into Winslow Road. Now walk into Frank Banfield Park (right). From here Chancellors Road leads us along, left, to the riverside. Go right here, with views across the river to the Harrods Depository, where quality furniture and items were stored.

We are now on the Thames Path (north side). Passing the Chancellor's and the City Arms pubs. Hammersmith Bridge is a very ornate bridge, with much detail. Cross over Hammersmith Bridge Road (with care) and note the crest on the bridge depicting the coats of arms of Kent, Surrey, Westminster, Essex, Middlesex, the City of London and the initials of the Metropolitan Board of Works, (M.B.W.). This striking bridge was constructed to a design by the great engineer Joseph Bazalgette, in 1882, replacing the first bridge of 1827,- by William Tierney Clarke, a replica of the bridge at Marlow. Now continue along the Thames Path at Lower Mall, Hammersmith.

MAP

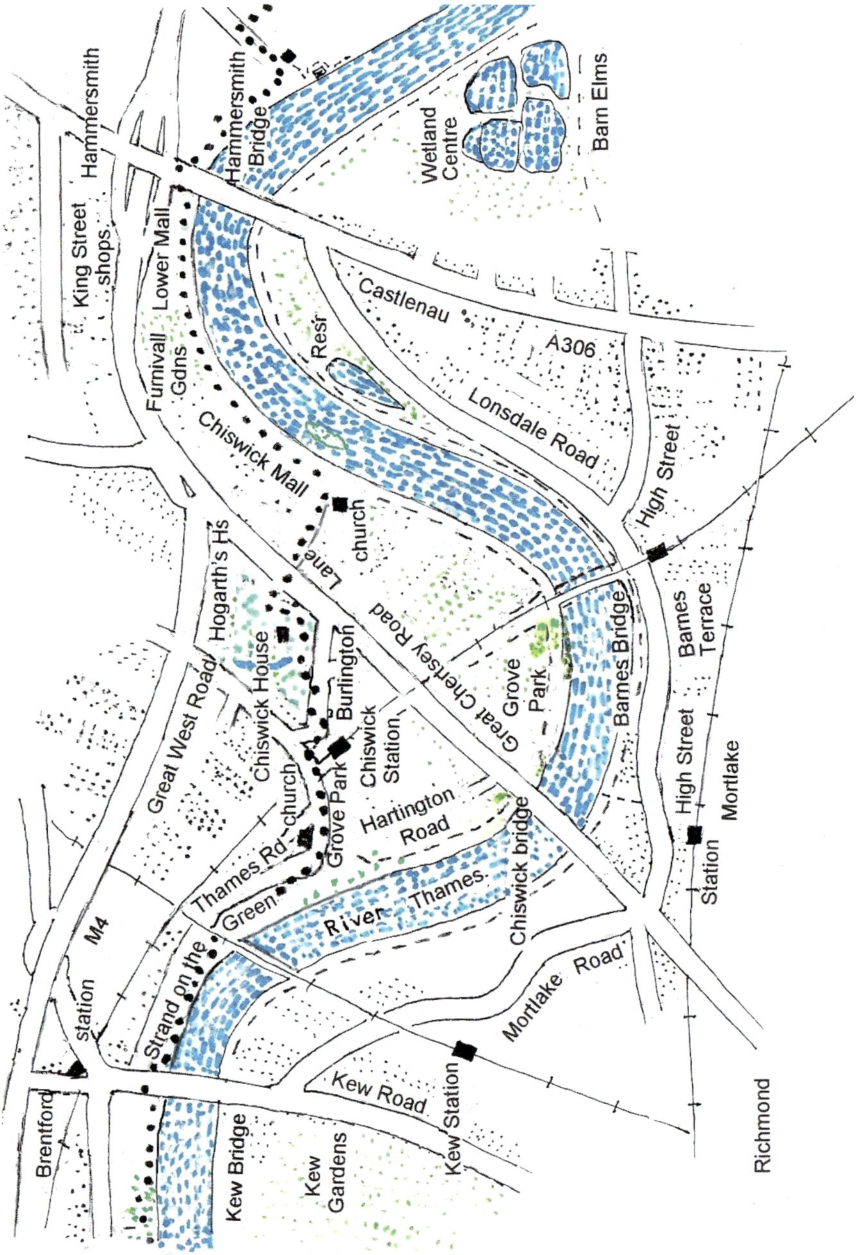
Hammersmith
King Street shops
Lower Mall
Furnivall Gdns
Hammersmith Bridge
Wetland Centre
Barn Elms
Castlenau
A306
Lonsdale Road
Resr
Chiswick Mall
church
Lane
Hogarth's Hs
Chiswick House
Burlington
Great Chertsey Road
Grove Park
High Street
Barnes Bridge
Barnes Terrace
High Street
Mortlake
Station
Great West Road
church
Grove Park
Chiswick Station
Hartington Road
Thames Rd
Green
River Thames
Chiswick bridge
M4
Strand on the
station
Mortlake Road
Brentford
Kew Bridge
Kew Gardens
Kew Road
Kew Station
Richmond

HAMMERSMITH TO KEW BRIDGE

Hammersmith Bridge and showing the county and city crests, right

Several public houses are passed, as this is a popular location. The first of these is the Blue Anchor, first recorded in 1722. Next door is The Rutland Arms. Followed by the large expanse of Furnivall Gardens, opened to the public in 1951. The lawned area, popular for relaxing on sunny days, was named after Dr.Frederick Furnivall, founder of the Furnivall Sculling Club in 1896. Further along is the old Quaker burial ground. The 18th century Meeting House was destroyed by a dreaded V1 Flying Bomb in july 1944. These rockets were aimed at London, with just enough fuel to reach their target and when the engine cut out, they fell from the sky, causing great devastation.

Turning left, we pass along a narrow alley beside The Dove, another old pub mentioned in 1792, where it is claimed, that Thomas Arne composed the music to 'Rule Brittania'.

The Thames Path at Lower Mall

Furnivall Gardens and 'The Dove'

Walking beside the Thames. Below: Chiswick Eyot (island)

St Nicholas's church, Chiswick

From the Black Lion pub, walk along the road past the river at Chiswick Eyot (island). This road is liable to flooding when the tide is high. Soon we reach St Nicholas's Church, Chiswick. The stone tower of this medieval church dates from 1486, but it was largely rebuilt in 1882. Here you will find the railed tomb and information about the famous artist, William Hogarth. Also buried here, in unmarked graves are Mary and Frances, daughters of Oliver Cromwell. It is also believed that his grave is here too. After his death, he was shamed and beheaded.

To the right of the church, walk along the footpath, Powell's Walk, which leads along, between narrow walls to Burlington Lane, opposite the gates to the park at Chiswick House. Use the crossing to enter the park. Hogarth's House is to the right and is worth a visit,. A drinking trough bears the words 'Be kind and merciful to your animals'. But we head left to Chiswick House.. The front of the house is a remarkable sight and the house and the various features are a real highlight of this walk. The gardens include a narrow, canal -shaped lake.

Chiswick House and the'Obelisk'

Chiswick House was built for the 3rd Duke of Burlington in 1725-29 and was based on Palladino's Villa Rotunda in Vicenza. The original Jacobean mansion was demolished in 1758. Walk down, passing the fountain and waterfall. From the obelisk gate, exit and turn right, walking along the lower part of Burlington Lane toward Chiswick Station. Walk past the entrance and go up the steps, crossing the railway bridge, left. This leads us to Grove Park Road and along to St Paul's Church. At the end, proceed along , right, to reach the narrow road and the Thames waterside at Strand-on the-Green, noted for its pubs and good food - The Bull's Head, City Barge and the Bell and Crown.

The steps leading up to Grove Park Road.
Below: Thames Road, leading to Strand-on the-Green

MAP

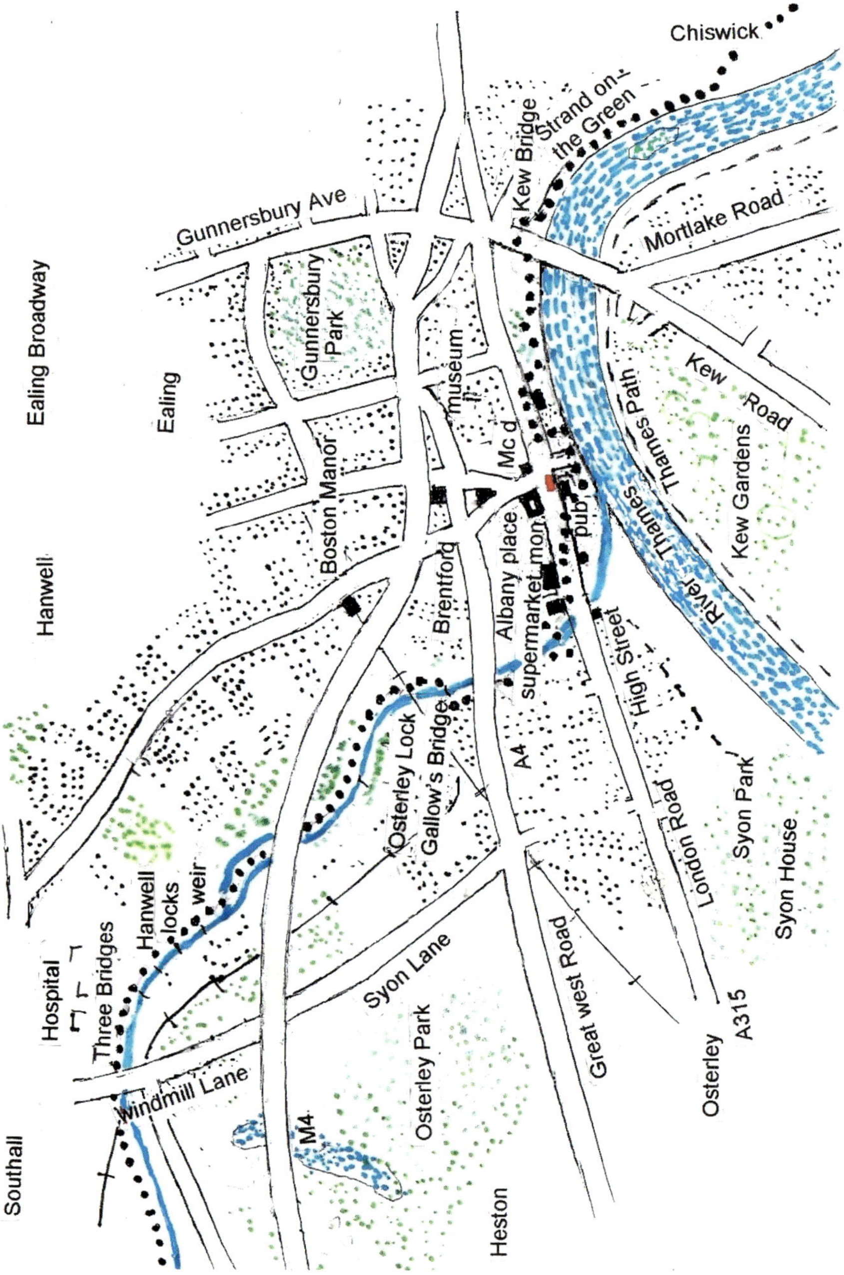
Chiswick
Strand on the Green
Kew Bridge
Gunnersbury Ave
Mortlake Road
Gunnersbury Park
Ealing Broadway
Ealing
museum
Kew Road
Thames Path
Mc d
Boston Manor
Kew Gardens
River Thames
pub
Albany place
mon
supermarket
Brentford
Hanwell
High Street
A4
Osterley Lock
Gallow's Bridge
London Road
Syon Park
Syon House
weir
Hanwell locks
Three Bridges
Hospital
Syon Lane
Great west Road
A315
Osterley
Osterley Park
Windmill Lane
M4
Southall
Heston

KEW BRIDGE TO EALING

Kew Bridge

Once across Kew Bridge, we are now in Brentford, part of the London borough of Hounslow. At one time it was the county town of the former county of Middlesex - now part of Greater London. Beyond the modern Regatta Port Apartments, note the elaborately styled chimney of the old water pumping station, which once supplied a great part of west London with water. There is now a museum here. Before us the Thames Path continues past riverboats, then up steps and along a road, then a lawned area, Waterman's Park, with picnic tables.

We now reach Brentford High Street, with shops, food outlets and hotels. Go around the dock - side, left, passing The Waterman pub, at the point where the Grand Union Canal flows into the Thames. The restored red and grey brick building is named Peerless Pumps and dated 1704. we are led around a dock basin, then back to the High Street near the supermarket.

Top: The water pumping station tower. Below: Waterman's Park, Brentford.

The Peerless Pumps Building

On the corner of the High Street and Alexandra Road, near the County Court stands the Brentford Monument (a slight detour, back). A pillar, once part of the old Brentford Bridge, - replaced by Kew Bridge, was 're-discovered' under industrial and coal waste in 1909. The inscription mentions Julius Caesar's crossing the Thames in 54 B.C., King Offa's church council meeting and Edmund Ironside, the Saxon King driving Canute and the Danes, back across the Thames in 1016.

Cross the road, then, near the Beehive pub and the Magistrates Courts, go right towards the lock basin, at Tallow Road. Cross the bridge, with views of the canal and new buildings, turning left. Go up and across the little footbridge, then around to the right where we pass the narrow boats. We are now walking alongside the canal. Proceed through the boat repair paint workshop and loading bay and continue along the towpath. Passing under a wooden bridge and under the Great Western Road (A4), our towpath takes us over Gallows Bridge - note the letters GJC (Grand Junction Canal) and the date,1820.

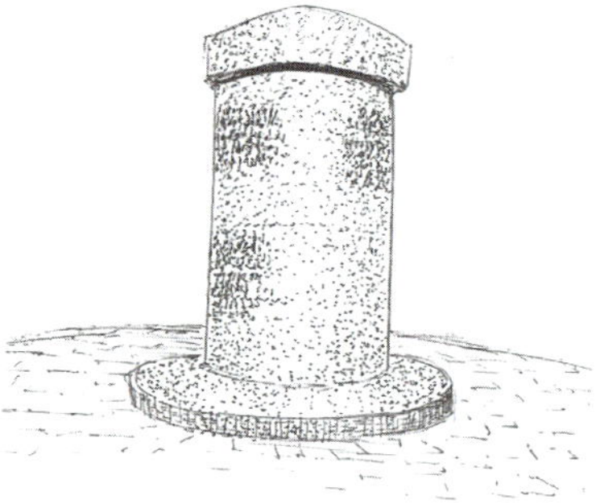

The Monument (right) and the canal basin at Brentford.

The canal was constructed between 1790 and 1820 and was originally known as the Grand Junction Canal. It was built between Braunston in Northamptonshire and Brentford. This was the boom time for canal building, with plans being passed for the construction of 20 canals across the country. Before the railways came, goods were mainly transported by barge and greatly contributed to prosperity at the time of the industrial revolution. Heavy loads could be carried at relative ease in comparison to the various tracks and turnpikes, which were often steep, rutted and muddy.

The footbridge over the canal, Brentford.
Below: Near the start of the canal and the GSK building.

We are now on the right side of the canal, which you follow all the way to the Slough arm, some seven miles distant. The girder bridge, ahead, carries the Piccadilly Line near Boston Manor Station. This part was constructed in the 1920s. The sound of traffic hurrying along the M4 is heard as we approach, then pass under the motorway bridge. Elthorne Park and Waterside are natural areas for observing wildlife, perhaps even the water vole, now much rarer than formerly. Many birds can be seen along the canal and these include ducks, moorhen, coot, great crested and little grebe and cormorants. At times it is hard to believe that we are well within the bounds of London, but the occasional sound of motor vehicles and aircraft flying to and from Heathrow Airport may remind us.

Gallows Bridge

The Piccadilly Line railway bridge

Several small waterfalls tumble down the weir where the Brent River is taken off. A large industrial factory and associated buildings are seen on the opposite side, after which the towpath leads us along a pleasant, leafy section. Passing St. Margaret's open space, Ealing, a sign points to the Fox pub, right. A series of lock gates add to the interest. Hanwell Locks opened in 1794. A finger post here shows the distances in miles to various places - Bulls Bridge 2 3/4, Uxbridge 8 3/4, Rickmansworth 16 and Birmingham 136 1/2. This part of London takes us through the areas of Hanwell, Ealing and Southall, although the leafy banks of the canal are predominant throughout.

The weir, River Brent.
The Grand Union Canal and lock, West Ealing.

The locks and the wall at Ealing Hospital

A long, high wall on our right encloses Ealing Hospital. This was once an asylum for mentally ill patients and the notice tells us that the bricked up archways were once doorways used to transport various goods to and from the barges.

Life on the canals, now an idyllic way of life, was not always easy. Families lived in cramped conditions on the narrow boats. Lock keepers were kept busy, especially on the 'stairs' where there were many lock gates. As it often took several hours to pass through, queues formed and some boatmen became impatient and angry as they waited to deliver their cargo. So, the less locks, the quicker their progress was made, but obviously locks were needed where there were gradients.

MAP

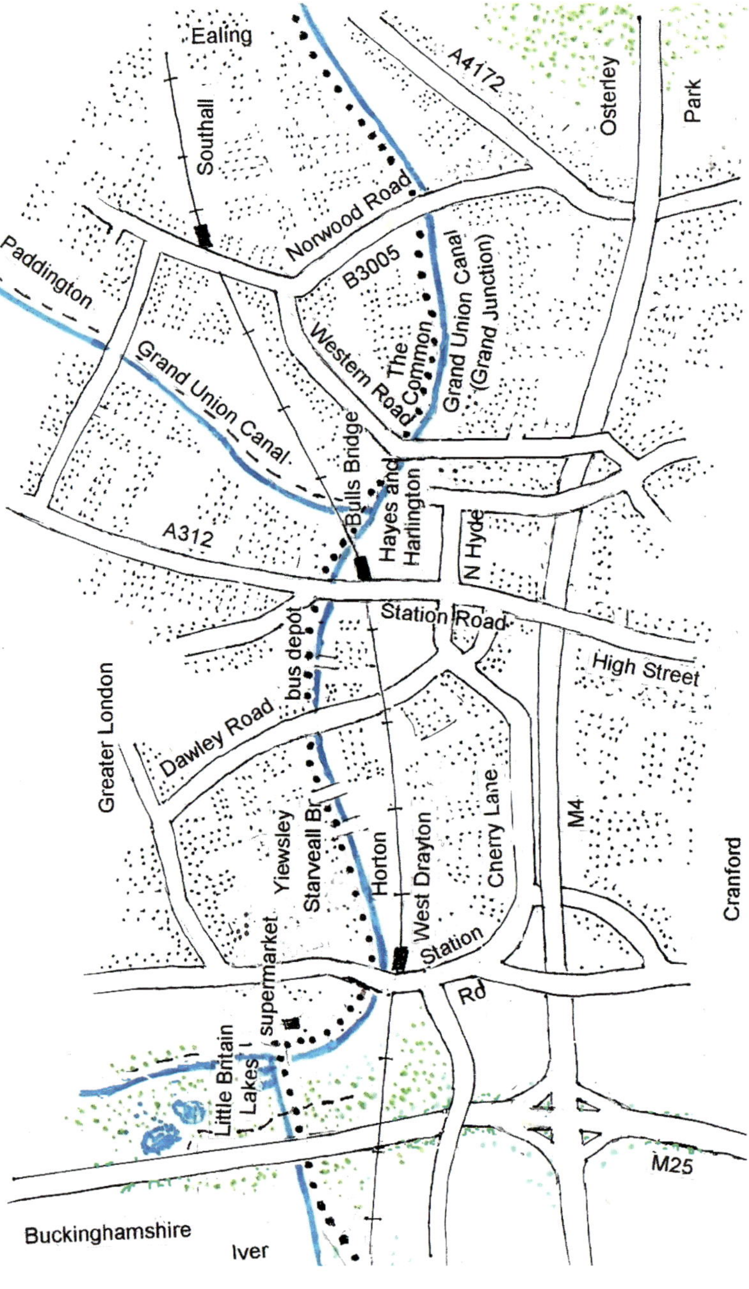
Ealing
A4172
Osterley
Park
Southall
Norwood Road
To Paddington
B3005
Grand Union Canal
(Grand Junction)
Western Road
The Common
Grand Union Canal
Bulls Bridge
Hayes and Harlington
A312
N Hyde
Station Road
High Street
bus depot
Dawley Road
Greater London
Cherry Lane
M4
Yiewsley
Starveall Br
Horton
West Drayton
Station
Cranford
Rd
supermarket
Little Britain Lakes
M25
Buckinghamshire
Iver

EALING TO IVER

The next point of interest is Windmill Bridge (or Three Bridges), where the canal and towpath pass above a railway line and beneath a road. Protecting the brickwork is an iron edge piece. Note the grooves formed long ago over many years, - made by the ropes connecting the horses to the barges and narrow boats. The bridge was re-constructed and became the last undertaking of the famous Victorian engineer Isambard Kingdom Brunel, in 1859 (along with the famous Royal Albert Bridge over the River Tamar between Plymouth and Cornwall). The canal is carried across the railway line by means of a trough- like iron aqueduct.

The Grand Union Canal at Southall

The Old Oak Tree

We are now 90 miles from Braunston and some 40 miles from Oxford. A road running parallel, on the right is called The Common. The pubs are named The Old Oak Tree and The Grand Junction Arms, between which Western Road, Southall, passes over us. The path goes along a roadway and on the canal here, boats are moored. We are soon led along to Bull's Bridge, where the Grand Union Canal joins our Brentford arm. The London Loop path also joins our towpath at this point. Ahead, a wide low bridge takes us under Brunel's famous straight, fast railway line from Paddington to Reading and the west. The next bridge carries the A312 over the canal. Hayes Bus Depot and also a huge factory are passed. Keep left at a fork.

This region is West Drayton and Yiewsley and along with Iver and Slough became a major brick making area. The bricks made from the clay and gravel of this area were used for the numerous houses and other buildings of London.

Above: Bulls Bridge, where the Harrow and Paddington canal branches off.
Below: Near Horton Bridge Road

A white bridge carries Horton Lane over and soon after, another bridge, the A408. here the canal swings to the north towards Uxbridge. New developments and a superstore, right, are seen here.

We soon leave the Grand Union Canal and join the Slough arm. (A minor extension for the transporting of bricks to London and one of the last canals to be constructed). A girder footbridge takes us across, left. From the bridge there are views along the canals and also over the marina. Continue walking along the towpath. A footbridge leads over the canal, this is Trout Lane and leads to the old gravel pits, now known as Little Britain Lakes. However, we continue straight on, under the M25 motorway then up the path left, to join Thorney Lane near Iver Station. Here we carefully cross the road, turning right, walking along the pavement towards Iver village.

Modern apartments at West Drayton

The footbridge leading to the Slough canal, left. Below: The canal boat marina

MAP

M25
church
Inn
Delaford Pk
Thorney Lane
Iver
Slough Canal
station
Love Green
Iver Heath
Uxbridge Road
Pinewood Studios
Black Park
Bellswood Lane
M40
Fulmer Rise
church
pub
Fulmer
A412
Temple Gdns
Langley Park
Blackpark Rd
George Green
Stoke Common
Frame Wood
B416
Temple Lane
Stoke Poges
Slough

IVER TO FULMER

Along the path - the M25 bridge beyond.
Below: St. James' church, Iver

Iver, formerly Evreham (Homestead on the hill), is recorded in the Domesday Survey of 1086. by 1351 Iver was granted a Royal Charter to hold weekly markets. As we approach, notable landmarks are the church, 12th century, with a 16th century tower and the Swan Inn. Turn left here at the High Street and walk past the Bull pub and shops including a bakery. Use the crossing near the recreation ground and pass the Iver Board School. Where the road bends left, go right along a footpath - lined with nettles - and then across a field.

The Swan Inn, Iver

Iver Board School

At the minor road, go left, then right at Love Green. Cross over to the pavement and continue along the bridleway, left. The path goes past fences and under the overhanging fir trees. Cross busy Wood Lane by using the island in the centre and walk in into Bellswood Lane. Cross the next road and after a large modern house, Treal Farm, we are led along to Langley Country Park. This is a beautiful park with many fine specimens of trees and shrubs. Go right here, walking up an avenue of mighty pines and fir trees. We approach the tea rooms at Temple Gardens, which is particularly impressive in the spring, with a colourful display of rhododendrons and azaleas. (From Iver we have been following the route of the Beeches Way and the Shakespeare Way paths and continue to do so as far as the Thames Path at Cookham).

The footpath leaving Iver. Below: Bellswood Lane

Mighty trees - Langley Park. Below: The Tea Rooms

From the tea rooms in Langley Park, we keep left through Temple Gardens and follow the path to the Uxbridge Road, (A412), a very busy dual carriageway. Great care is needed when crossing. Use the central reservation and be patient, especially if you are in a group or with younger members. A footbridge here would be helpful.

Late spring in Temple Gardens, Langley Park

Once we have negotiated this road, we are in Black Park where another treat awaits us. Go left along a wide track called Rhododendron Drive, keeping right at the end brings us to the cafe and the play area. The beautiful vistas of Blackpark Lake opens out before us;-the water covers a considerable area and the entire park covers 620 acres. We go left around the lake walking along a wide gravel path with seats at various viewpoints. The usual water birds are seen here, including swans, coot and moorhen. Black Park lies near Pinewood Studios and this location has been used for many well known films, including James Bond's Goldfinger and the park and the lake have often been featured in both film and TV productions.

The track leading along to Black Park and the café (below)

Views of Blackpark Lake

We continue around the edge and when we reach the head of Blackpark Lake, go straight on, past an area of heath land and past an adventure/ orienteering course. After 200 yards (about 180 metres) , where the paths divide, bear left, then right soon after (sign posted Beeches Way). Next turn left onto a footpath, muddy at first which leads to a stile and a minor road. Go right here, walking along the road. On reaching the junction ahead, turn left along the next road. Cross over and turn right onto the footpath at Fulmer Rise.

The path leaving Black Park

Rhododendrons near Fulmer Rise and (below) along the footpath

From the houses at Fulmer Rise, follow the road, then keep left along the footpath and at the next crossing go straight on. The footpath now leads us behind fences and past more rhododendrons (colourful in the late spring). We now cross a field with a fence beside the path. From the far corner follow the Beeches Way which leads us to a stile and across a field (beware of electric fences!), bearing right past the stables to arrive at the village of Fulmer. On the left is St. James' Church - the red brickwork contrasts markedly with the grey stone of Iver Church, which we passed a few miles before.

The path nearing Fulmer

MAP

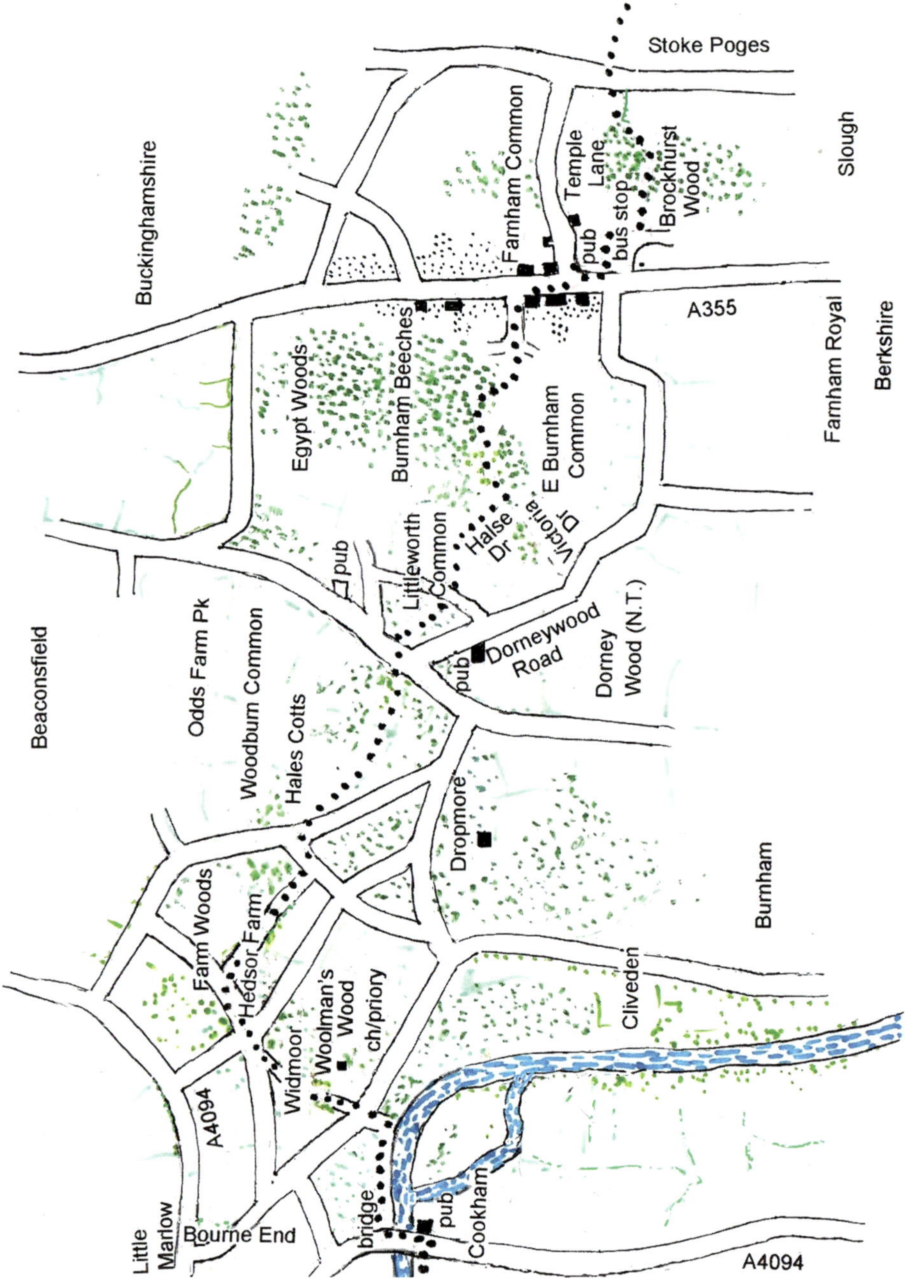
Stoke Poges
Slough
Buckinghamshire
Farnham Common
Temple Lane
Brockhurst Wood
pub
bus stop
A355
Farnham Royal
Berkshire
Egypt Woods
Burnham Beeches
E Burnham Common
Halse Dr
Victoria Dr
Littleworth Common
pub
Beaconsfield
Odds Farm Pk
Woodburn Common
Hales Cotts
pub
Dorneywood Road
Dorney Wood (N.T.)
Dropmore
Burnham
Farm Woods
Hedsor Farm
Woolman's Wood
ch/priory
Cliveden
Widmoor
A4094
Little Marlow
Bourne End
bridge
pub
Cookham
A4094

FULMER TO COOKHAM

St James' Church and attractive old cottages, Fulmer

The Black Horse pub

Keep left here, walking up the hill and where the road forks keep right, cross with care and walk up this road. Soon a footpath is encountered, left. Go along the path, through a wooded area, then out onto the heath at Stoke Common. The moorland area provides another contrast to this varied walk. The path leads straight across the heath, passing a little pond surrounded by small trees. The trees in these parts are mainly willow and birch and typically beech and oak in the woodland areas. At the next paths, keep right and carefully cross the road and continue ahead. A notice here tells us that the common is owned by the City of London.

On Stoke Common. Below: Approaching Brockhurst Wood

We now cross another road and go across the field. At the gate turn left, where we find a firm path that swings around through the edge of Brockhurst Wood. Turn right at the next junction where there is a good gravel path. Go over the stile to pass through a pleasant wooded section, then over a little brick footbridge. Passing through Ingram's Copse there is a dense area of laurel and holly, which soon leads us to the road at Farnham, Buckinghamshire.

Go right, past the village hall and the Victoria pub. At the main road, with the Forester's public house on the corner, turn right, using the crossing, pass the shops, - which includes a cafe and fish and chips, a pub, the Stag and Hounds and an Indian restaurant. Now turn left along Beeches Road, for the forest at Burnham Beeches. Crossing a road we walk over a grassy area, with a car park to our left. This is another local beauty spot. The trees are mostly beech and oak.

Walking through Brockhurst Wood

The Foresters at Farnham Below: Beeches Road

In Burnham Beeches - a famous National Trust forest

The notice board at Burnham Beeches

Now enter the forest by following the path, right. This leads over a little brook. Bearing left, soon we reach a road and ahead is a forest track called Victoria Drive. Don't go this way, instead go right and up the tarmac road. This is named Halse Drive. go straight ahead and along Morton Drive. From the Corporation of London notice board, at the minor road, go right, then turn left following the Shakespeare Way and the Beeches Way path. Keep to the path and opposite Dimsdale, go right. This is part of the Portman Burtley Estate.

Along the path Below: Crossing Littleworth Common

Cross the next road keeping to the Beeches Way. At the next fork, keep going straight ahead and enter a field - the path leads us between fences. In this area, red kites, (large birds of prey) are frequently seen - here and over the Chilterns it is estimated that there are well over 500 pairs.

Again we cross over another road - do not go along the bridle track, left, instead cross the little car park to the path, which leads us across Littleworth Common - a very pleasant area of open country and heath. Cross Dorneywood Road, go right - then left, crossing the road, (with care) to the footpath opposite. Follow the path between a fence and a hedge, going along a track through a nice wooded section.

A farmer harvesting near Hedsor

A track leading to a road near Farm Woods

Again, carefully cross another road, going into a dense wood with rhododendrons. Cross the next road, following the driveway, opposite and past a quaint little cottage. The narrow footpath ahead is often muddy as we pass along the edge of the woods. Continue by going left, along the road, keeping to the verge. Farm Woods, opposite, is a haven for wildlife including roe deer, mandarin ducks and dormice. The picnic tables provide a good place to have a break.

Keep walking along the roadside, passing a row of red brick houses and Hedsor Place. Go straight on keeping to the verge to avoid the traffic. At the right bend, our route goes straight on, along Branch Lane and past a large, red brick house, Hedsor Farm. The footpath bears left along a track and the path now continues to the right of a fence. (Not into Woolmans Wood). The various types of trees include holly and ash, which here grow tall and straight. A good path, beside railings leads down to the road. On the hill above is the 11th century St. Nicholas Church. (A path goes up to the left).

Farm Woods (above) and Hedsor Farm

A footpath leading up to Hedsor Church and the houses at the Quay

Crossing a footbridge on nearing the Thames at Cookham

Cross the main road between Bourne End and Burnham and pass through a gate leading down to the big houses at the quay. Keep right, walking between the walls, passing through another gateway and onto a footbridge, which takes us over a shady little stream. We keep left, along the edge of a field, which leads us back to the River Thames for the first time since Brentford.

The route now takes us across the field to Cookham. Turn left along the roadside and walk over the bridge that crosses the Thames. The bridge, supported by seven pairs of iron legs, was constructed in 1867. A popular pub, The Ferry, offers drinks and good food. Built in 1354 its original name was "The Ford". Expensive houses, with gardens and boat moorings line the banks of the river. One boathouse is the office of the Keeper of the Royal swans and the tradition of 'swan upping' takes place every year to count and mark all the cygnets. Cookham was also the home of the renowned artist, Stanley Spencer.

MAP

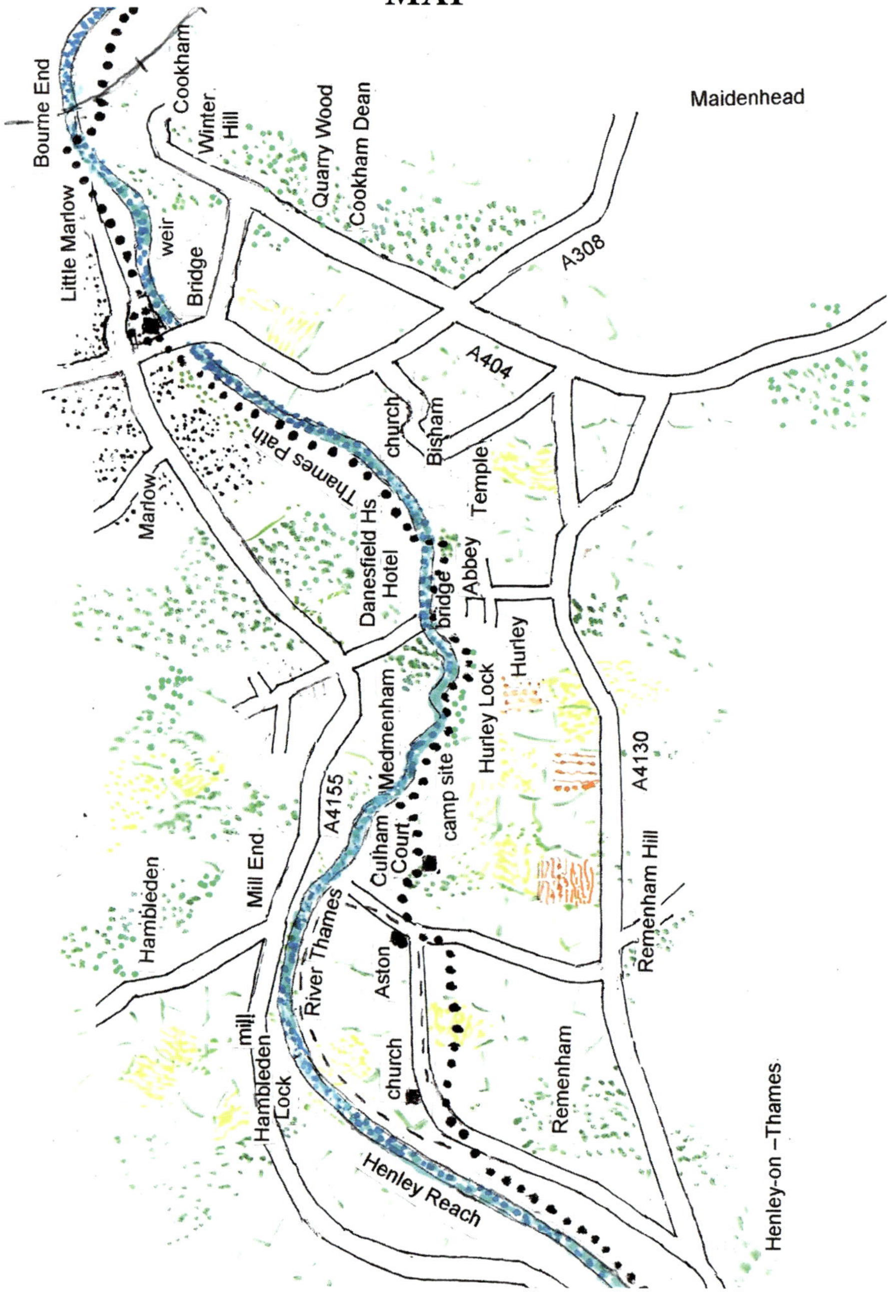
Bourne End
Cookham
Winter Hill
Quarry Wood
Cookham Dean
Maidenhead
Little Marlow
weir
Bridge
A308
A404
church
Bisham
Thames Path
Marlow
Temple
Danesfield Hs Hotel
Abbey
bridge
Hurley
Hurley Lock
Medmenham
camp site
A4155
A4130
Culham Court
Mill End
Hambleden
Remenham Hill
River Thames
Aston
mill
Hambleden Lock
church
Remenham
Henley Reach
Henley-on –Thames

COOKHAM TO MARLOW AND HENLEY- ONTHAMES

On Cookham Bridge, with the church beyond

From Cookham Bridge, go down the steps, right, to the Thames Path at Bell Rope Meadow. Here, strands of string or twine, were twisted together to make rope. A long narrow strip of land was needed to make a continuous length of rope. From here, a tarmac path takes us past Cookham Reach Sailing Club. A grass path, through National Trust land, with the remnants of ancient man, now heads towards the Bourne End railway bridge, which we pass under. Go up the steps and across the pedestrian walkway, to reach the path on the north side of the river. Stations here at Cookham, Bourne End and Marlow link to the main line at Maidenhead.

Views of the River Thames at Cookham

The Railway Bridge and the footbridge near Bourne End

Proceed along a narrow path between gardens with views across the Bounty pub. On our side is the OTT bar and restaurant, where you may also obtain ice cream and cold drinks We stay on the path but just inland a footpath leads to Little Marlow and the Country Park. There are seven lakes and activities range from water sports, fishing and bird watching. It is claimed that well over 200 species of birds have been observed here. The Thames Path continues along the riverside as we head towards Marlow.

Looking across the river to the 'Bounty' and near Little Marlow (below)

Meanwhile , we now cross a meadow, with a railway line to Marlow, right. This area of houses with well tended gardens and weeping willows, now gives way to more natural tree lined banks. Lombardy poplar trees and steep wooded shores opposite, is the location for more large, exclusive homes. These banks, located between Winter Hill and Quarry Wood, were the inspiration for Kenneth Grahame's " Wind in the Willows", featuring "Ratty", "Mole" and "Toad of Toad Hall".

Next, a picnic area with seats is passed and leads us under the bridge that carries the busy A404 road. At another pleasant seating area, swing right and away from the river. We are now in Marlow. Go left and along the roadside with views to the bridge and the lofty spire of Marlow church.

'Wind in the willows' at Quarry Wood

A castle-like property on the river.
Below: A view of beautiful Marlow

The Two Brewers pub

After about 200 metres and a right bend, the Thames Path goes left - a narrow path between brick walls. The Two Brewers pub, right, is dated 1755, but parts date from Tudor times. Our path continues ahead, across the road and soon we encounter All Saints Church, a building of grand size, the tower and spire being particularly imposing. One notable memorial is to Sir Miles Hobart, who, in 1628, changed certain tax laws in parliament.

All Saints Church, Marlow

The suspension bridge, a reminder of the old Hammersmith Bridge, was built by William Tierney Clark in 1831 - 1836 and was renovated in 1966. Here in Marlow, the Crown Hotel was once frequented by Dick Turpin, the notorious highwayman. Marlow has also been home to many writers and poets including T.S. Elliot and Jerome K. Jerome. In Albion House, West Street, lived Mary Shelley and it was here that she wrote her classic gothic story " Frankenstein".

Instead of crossing Marlow Bridge, go down to the right and follow the Thames Path. A wide green space, Court Garden, is often very busy during the summer months - people relaxing, groups, families and even wedding parties. The Marlow regatta takes place in June, when this area is particularly busy. The path continues with little footbridges crossing streams.

The suspension bridge. Below: The waterfront at Marlow

All Saints Church, Bisham

On the opposite side of the river lies Bisham. In the twelfth century an abbey was built here by the Knights Templar, a medieval order who protected pilgrims visiting the Holy Land. Little remains of the abbey today, but All Saints Church, with its Norman Tower is well seen from our side of the river.

Beside the path a memorial stone here remembers Giles Every of Marlow, who was killed in a boating accident during the 1984 regatta. At Temple, keep to the right of the lock keeper's hut. Our path now crosses the river by a high, arched bridge. Walking steeply up, we have great views of the Thames Valley and river, from the top. Once over the bridge, we walk beneath the boughs of horse chestnut trees as we approach the islands of Hurley Lock. A footbridge takes us onto one of the islands and soon after another bridge, also with concrete treads takes us off the island.

The high arched footbridge and the view upstream to Hurley Lock

This pleasant location is near Hurley, another village of historical interest. A Norman church and the ruins of an earlier Saxon church are found here. There are also ruins of a Benedictine Monastery and a mansion. It is claimed that Edith, the sister of Edward the Confessor is buried here at Hurley. The old tavern, called Ye Old Bell Inn, is one of the oldest pubs and dates from 1135. Across the river, on the north shore, the Norman's built an abbey - it too fell into disuse, but was rebuilt by Sir Francis Dashwood-of the Hellfire Club notoriety- as a grand home overlooking the River Thames.

Leaving Hurley Lock

On the island at Hurley

A wide grass area here leads us along, with willow and alder trees lining the side, then a holiday park and camp site with static homes is passed on our left. Continuing through a small private wood, then across fields, the route leads us back to the riverside - we are now midway between Marlow and Henley and the area is often quiet. After crossing other fields and footbridges, the path turns left and reaches a minor road.

Culham Court.
Below: The Flower Pot Hotel

From the road, keep right, walking up the track with views to Culham Court, a large mansion. Wild flowers grow in abundance here, these include blue geraniums, scabious, mallow and ladies mantle. The little hamlet, ahead, is called Aston. Go right, along the road that leads to the Flower Pot Hotel. From here either follow the Thames Path, down, right, or follow the road, (or footpath) left, which leads to Remenham. The former leads to the Thames at Hambleden Lock and Mill, dating from1338. whereas following the road is quicker. The footpath is found after Highway Cottage, on the right.

Remenham has a notable church, with its lych gate and memorials. Walking on, past the Upper Thames Rowing Club and over a little humped bridge, we are now nearing Henley on Thames - the bridge and church coming into view.

Passing Remenham Church

MAP

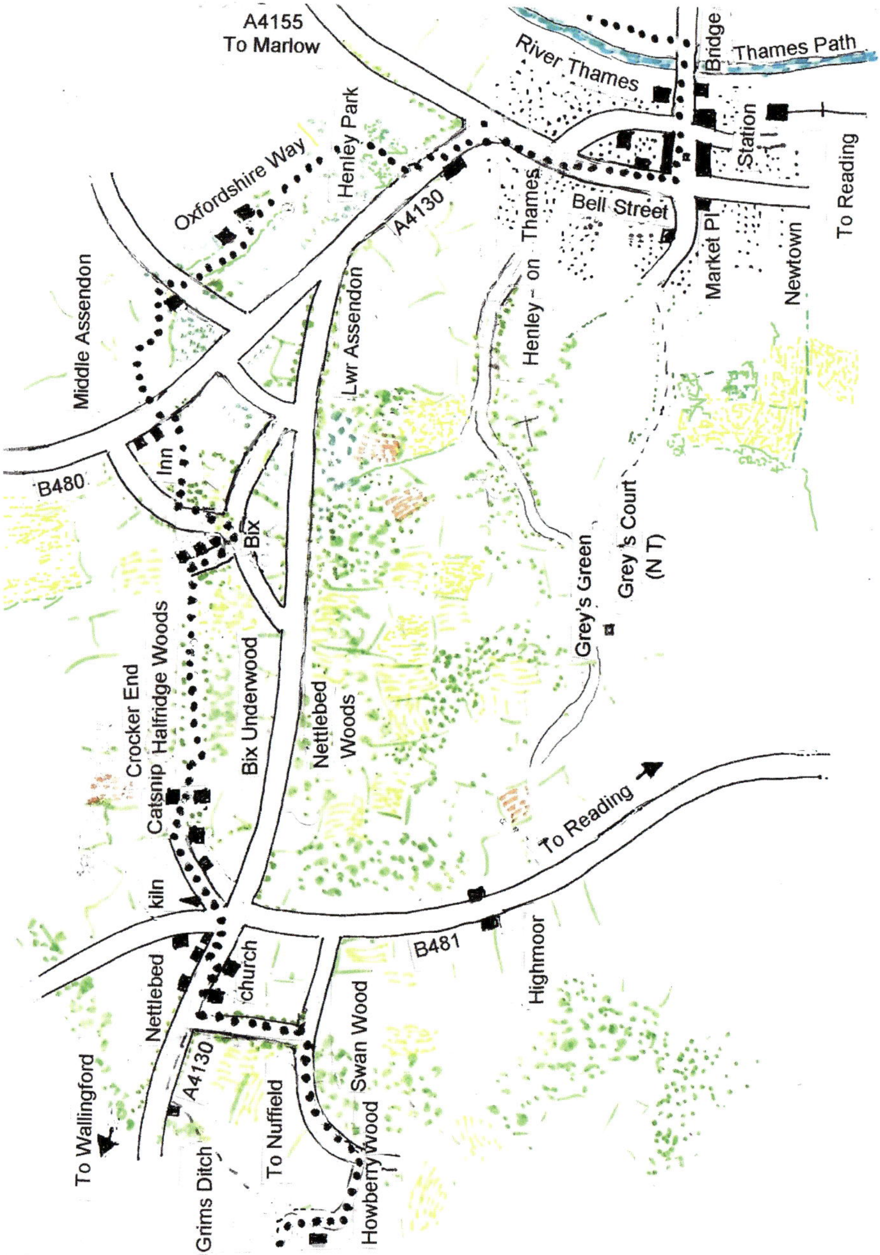
A4155
To Marlow
River Thames
Bridge
Thames Path
Henley Park
Oxfordshire Way
Station
To Reading
A4130
Bell Street
Henley - on Thames
Market Pl
Newtown
Middle Assendon
Lwr Assendon
B480
Inn
Bix
Grey's Court
(N T)
Grey's Green
Crocker End
Halfridge Woods
Bix Underwood
Nettlebed
Woods
Catsnip
To Reading
kiln
B481
Highmoor
Nettlebed
church
Swan Wood
A4130
To Wallingford
Grims Ditch
To Nuffield
Howberry Wood

HENLEY - ON - THAMES TO NUFFIELD

Nearing Henley Bridge

Before we reach the bridge, on our left are the Leander Club and opposite, the Henley Royal Regatta Headquarters. The Leander Club is the world's oldest and most prestigious rowing club, founded in 1818. World and Olympic champions have trained here. The famous Henley Royal Regatta was founded in 1839 and takes place in July. It received Royal patronage, by Prince Albert in 1851.

We now step onto, and cross Henley Bridge, -a notice says that engine drivers are only permitted to take one load at a time across the bridge! The original bridge, (1234), an old stone structure, had a chapel and an inn. This was replaced by a wooden bridge, which was washed away by a flood in 1774. The present 5 arched bridge was built by William Hayward in 1786. The figures of Isis and Old Father Thames are seen above the central arch each side.

The Angel Inn and Henley Bridge, showing the 'Isis' figure

St. Mary's Church, Henley on Thames

The church, St. Mary's, dates back to the 12th century and was largely re-built in 1410. (The tower is 16th century). This is where, in 1999, the funeral of the famous 1960s pop/ soul singer Dusty Springfield took place. Another resident of Henley was the former Beatle guitarist George Harrison, who lived nearby. From the bridge, walk straight ahead, with the church, right and along Hart Street towards Market Place and the Town Hall. Go right along Bell Street. A supermarket and the cinema are along here. As we leave the town, at the mini roundabout, the road forks – right to Marlow and left to Nettlebed and Wallingford. Keep left, then cross over, walking past the Quakers meeting place and Fairmile Court. Here, a path goes up, right. This is the Oxfordshire Way, that takes us up over the Chiltern Hills.

Market Place.
Below: Leaving Henley - at the road junction, keep left.

Go steeply up and through the woods, avoiding other paths right and down, left. Keep walking up, past a row of hornbeam trees. Going through a kissing gate, we enter Deer Park and looking back have a delightful view over the Thames country near Henley.

Walking up the path from Henley.
Below: Crossing Deer Park.

The gateway at Henley Park

Keep straight on, through the gate, with Henley Park, right. A road and a stony track passes large pine trees and houses. At Pond Cottage, on the minor road, the footpath heads left along a grassy path between enclosures with horses. Striking blue chicory flowers are seen in the summer. The long grass, with its mix of various wild flowers, is part of the Turville Estate, a conservation area.

From our lofty viewpoint, looking ahead, we have a wonderful view over the Chiltern Hills - one of the highlights of the entire walk. Walking steeply down a grass path, more wild flowers add to the interest, as we approach the B480 road at Middle Assendon. Keeping right, cautiously cross the road to the Rainbow Inn opposite. To the left, a path goes across a field and up through the trees. Between here and Nuffield we leave the National and County long distance paths - like the Oxfordshire Way,- but the route this way is excellent.

A glorious view on a summer's day in the Chiltern Hills.
Below: The Rainbow Inn at Middle Assendon.

The path leading up from Middle Assendon.
Below: The church at Bix

A wooden fence is left, as we proceed up between conifers, a little road, White Lane is ahead - go up left, walking beneath the overhanging branches. At the top, an open space leads us across the grass to Bix, a small village. An attractive little red roofed church, St James' awaits. Turn right here and walk along the road passing the village hall. At Bix Common, go left for Nettlebed. We are led across a field, which is often planted with corn - oats, wheat or barley. Butterflies such as marbled white, comma and meadow brown are seen here. In the woods, trees include sweet (or edible) chestnut and oak. These give way to a forest of conifers. The path continues for 1½ miles to Nettlebed; mainly good, firm with a few muddy places.

At the houses nearing Catslip, keep right, past Yew Tree Cottage. Follow the stony lane, then at the junction, go right. Catslip and Sarneys are passed - now walk right, then left, along the road. Walnut Cottage looks attractive in spring, with its covering of wisteria.

Heading towards Bix Underwood

Passing attractive cottages as we approach Nettlebed

You have now reached Nettlebed, with its old kiln that towers over the houses. Bricks and tiles have been fired here and a notice tells of its history, including the record of 35,000 tiles being made for Wallingford Castle in 1365.

Historical finds in this area prove that it has been inhabited from pre-historic times. The A4130 road has been a track since ancient times, leading across the Chilterns from Henley to Oxford. In 1736, it was made into a turnpike (toll road) for the use of horses carriages and coaches.

Walk along the pavement of the High Street, right. Go along past the public house and the Village Club, which is home to the Nettlebed Folk Club. Here, local musicians and national folk singers regularly perform. Use the crossing to walk along the left side, reaching St. Bartholomew's Church. Early records show that the church dates from the 12th century, but was re-built in 1845.

The old brick kiln.
Below: The White Hart and the High Street.

St. Bartholomew's church, Nettlebed.

For simplicity, we now follow the farm track at The Bothy, left. (There is also a footpath leading from the main road beyond - see map). After passing through the gate and along the tarmac farm road, walk on to the next road. Turn right. This little road has a sinister name - Deadman's Lane - then up a short slope, left - Devil's Hill! Views back over Nettlebed embrace the rolling hills and open fields of South Oxfordshire.

Now head for Howberry Farm, right. The bridle track keeps right of the farm buildings. After following this lane the footpath from the A4130 joins from the right. Here we keep left, through the trees following the track to Nuffield, sometimes muddy in places, but becoming firmer. In the woods here there are some fine beech trees.

Howberry Farm. The path is to the right.
Below: The wooded path leading to Nuffield.

MAP

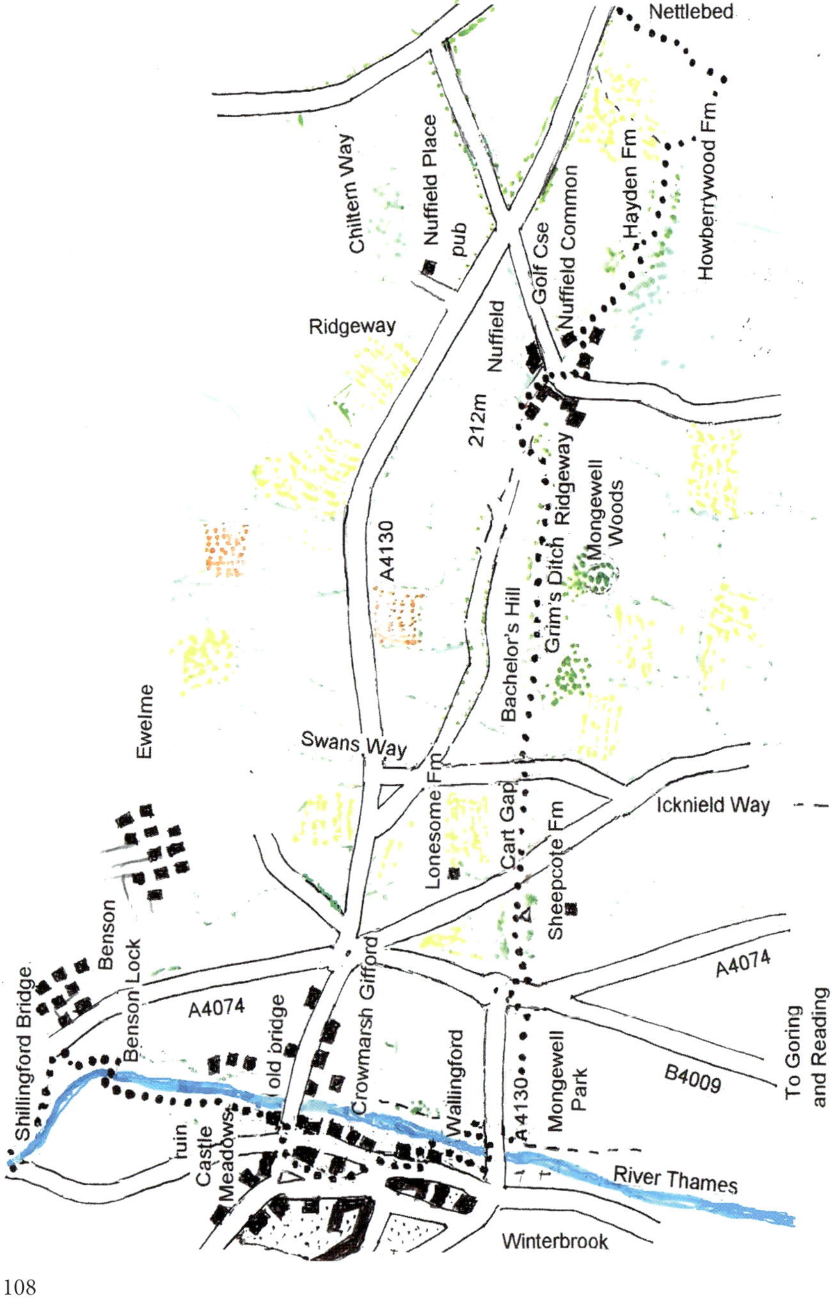
Nettlebed
Howberrywood Fm
Hayden Fm
Nuffield Common
Golf Cse
Chiltern Way
Nuffield Place
pub
Ridgeway
Nuffield
212m
Ridgeway
Mongewell
Woods
Grim's Ditch
Bachelor's Hill
A4130
Ewelme
Swans Way
Lonesome Fm
Cart Gap
Sheepcote Fm
Icknield Way
Benson
Benson Lock
Shillingford Bridge
A4074
old bridge
Crowmarsh Gifford
Wallingford
A4130
Mongewell
Park
A4074
B4009
To Goring
and Reading
ruin
Castle
Meadows
River Thames
Winterbrook

NUFFIELD TO WALLINGFORD

The church - with its wooden shingled tower

On reaching the houses at Nuffield, at Elderberry Cottage, go left along the path. Cautiously cross the road and walk along North Hill with the Huntercombe Golf Club, right. This road leads along, past the church, which kindly provides a drinking water tap. The flint stonework appears to be very old. The wooden tower is also a feature of many old English churches. Much of the church is 14th century, but parts of the Norman church remain, from around 1100.

The graveyard contains the burial place of William Morris, the engineer and car maker. In the aisle an inscription on a tomb reads: Edward Leaver (died) May ye 5th 1728, aged 82 years. From here, at the White House, a sign points to the left. We now join another celebrated ancient track, The Ridgeway, which took travellers along between Avebury, Wiltshire, to Ivinghoe Beacon in Buckinghamshire. Far away, in the flat, open countryside near Oxford, are the towers and chimneys of Didcot Power Station.

Keep right and follow The Ridgeway, left, down to a gateway where another water tap is provided. go through the gate, right. Here the path follows Grims Ditch, another very old historical feature. The ditch and the embankments are easily noticed in places, but be aware of some slippery slopes. Ancient Britons built these defensive positions. The Romans, who pushed north and west throughout the land, arrived here in about A.D. 43.

Finger Post on the Ridgeway. Below: Along Grim's Ditch

The Ridgeway at Cart Gap

Underfoot the soil is composed of chalk and flint. In the summer, the large blue blooms of the bellflower are abundant. In addition to the oak and beech trees which afforested much of the land in times long ago, the larch has established itself here. These are unusual in that they shed their needles for the winter, just as deciduous trees shed their leaves.

A little road, which we now cross follows the route of the Icknield Way - a pre-historic track across the chalk hills to the Norfolk coast. The next minor road is at Cart Gap, from where we have far reaching views across the Chiltern countryside and South Oxfordshire. A notice board here tells us that this is an area of outstanding natural beauty (A.O.N.B.). Following the path amidst the blackthorn and elderberry bushes, the O.S. Trig point, number S5729 is passed.

Grim's Ditch and the Ridgeway Path. The A 4074, left

We now reach the busy A4074 road that runs between Reading and Oxford. It is best negotiated to the right, where you can cross near the roundabout, using the central island. Go back, left, to the path opposite, which runs parallel with the A4130 into Wallingford. Where the paths go right and left, turn right and pass under the road. Turn up left to join the pavement that leads across the bridge. Once over, go down right, to join the Thames Path again, which takes us along into Wallingford.

After a little way, we go over a swing bridge at the Oxford University Boat Club. At the houses ahead, the Thames Path goes right, under a building and across a little bridge, soon joining St. Leonard's Lane. The church is partly Norman, but as is normally the case, mainly rebuilt. We are now in Wallingford. Turn right, walking past Wallingford Rowing Club and Castle Priory. At the car park, walk left under the arch and bear right into Hart Street, walking along to the town centre.

The River Thames near Wallingford.
Below: The O.U. Boat Club and footbridge.

MAP

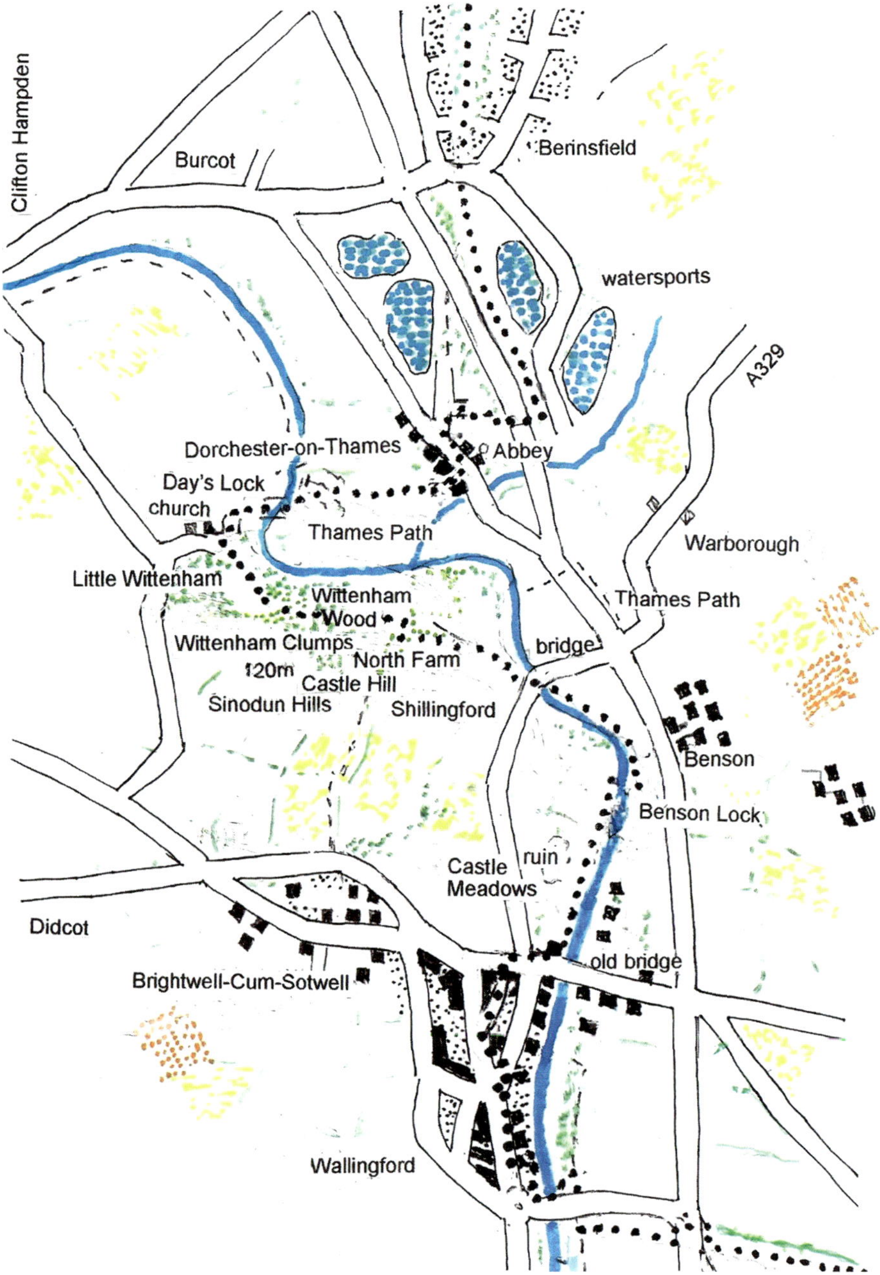
Clifton Hampden
Burcot
Berinsfield
watersports
A329
Dorchester-on-Thames
Abbey
Day's Lock
church
Thames Path
Warborough
Little Wittenham
Wittenham Wood
Thames Path
Wittenham Clumps
120m
North Farm
bridge
Castle Hill
Sinodun Hills
Shillingford
Benson
Benson Lock
Castle Meadows
ruin
Didcot
old bridge
Brightwell-Cum-Sotwell
Wallingford

WALLINGFORD TO DORCHESTER-ON-THAMES

St. Leonard's Church

Wallingford, a delightful old town, was one of the most important places in England and a Saxon stronghold. In 1066 William the Conqueror and his army marched through Wallingford and ordered a castle to be built. It became the largest walled town in England and in 1155 it was granted a charter by King Henry 1, which gave the town certain rights.

The wide, squat tower of St. Mary-Le-More comes into view. The tower was destroyed by lightning but was re-built in 1653. The church is medieval, but much of it now dates from 1854. The Market Place is a square at the centre. The old Town Hall contains the Tourist Information Centre.

Now, walk along the narrow, pedestrianised St. Mary's Street, which joins the High Street. Go right here. Opposite, is the George Hotel, bar and bistro, which has strange stories to tell. It is very old, dating back to the 1100s, but an early reference to the George is dated 1517. Dick Turpin, the highwayman, was also known to take refuge here.

Market Place, the Town Hall and St. Mary Le More Church, Wallingford.
Below: St. Mary's Street.

As we walk down, on the right is St. Peter's Church. It is also very old, but was destroyed in the civil war and it was re-built in 1769 with the ornate spire being added in 1777. this church contains the tomb of Sir William Blackstone (1780). His work was largely responsible for writing up the Declaration of Independence and the Constitution of the United States of America.

Go down to the riverside and Wallingford Bridge. A bar here is called The Boathouse -from where there is a a good view of the old medieval bridge, with its nineteen arches. After the great flood of 1809, which caused some damage, it was modified. From here, our Thames Path goes left, then right, to the riverside. The walking is good on a firm path, but it may become muddy as we proceed.

Wallingford Bridge

Castle Meadows. The ruins are just visible

On the right is the tranquil tree-lined river, while on the left are the Castle Meadows and the remains of the castle. It was the last stronghold of the Royalists during the civil war and because of this, it was ordered to be destroyed by Oliver Cromwell. Today it is in a very ruinous condition. Walking along we can hear the roar of the water as it tumbles down the weir at Benson Lock. This is a glorious place to linger on a warm and sunny day, perhaps sitting a while to take in the scene. The Lock Keeper's house is dated 1913, but the lock itself is much older, although it was re-constructed in 1870. Cross over the weir by means of the long, metal footbridge. At the car park, keep left along the road.

We are now alongside the A4074 road at Benson. St. Helen's Church tower is seen just above the trees. A church has stood here since 636, which was founded by St. Birinus. It was made famous by the German propaganda broadcaster Lord Haw Haw (William Joyce). He reported the bombing of the airfield near the village which has two elevens on the clock face in Roman numerals. (Nine should read IX not XI). Benson was the home of Reginald Lee who was born in 1870. Together, with Frederick Fleet, was a lookout on board the Titanic when the iceberg was spotted at 11:30 pm on the 14th April 1912. The lookouts survived the disaster, including those off-duty.

Benson Lock and the weir

The Waterfront Café

Turn left again through the gate, leading to an area with seats and a little swimming pool. The Waterfront Café is a popular place to stop for refreshments. Here, boats are moored at the marina and luxury chalets are passed. Go along with the meadow, right and through the wooded area with lime trees. Shillingford Bridge now comes into view and on the far side, the Shillingford Bridge Hotel bar and restaurant.

The foundations of the bridge approach have been re-enforced with bolts and plates - but it is strong enough to walk over! Cross the bridge and turn right, walking past the hotel and car park. This is another delightful location, with views of the river and the three central arches of the graceful bridge. Follow the North Farm road along and keep left at the farm gates.

From the pathway there are views across to the old Roman town of Dorchester and its abbey church. At the next junction, go right, then left along into the woods. The going is good throughout, except where forest vehicles have caused a rutted and muddy track. The nettles here attract certain butterflies such as the red admiral.

Shillingford Bridge and Hotel

**Looking across to Dorchester-on-Thames and its abbey church.
Below: Round Hill and Wittenham Clumps.**

The View from the Wittenham Clumps

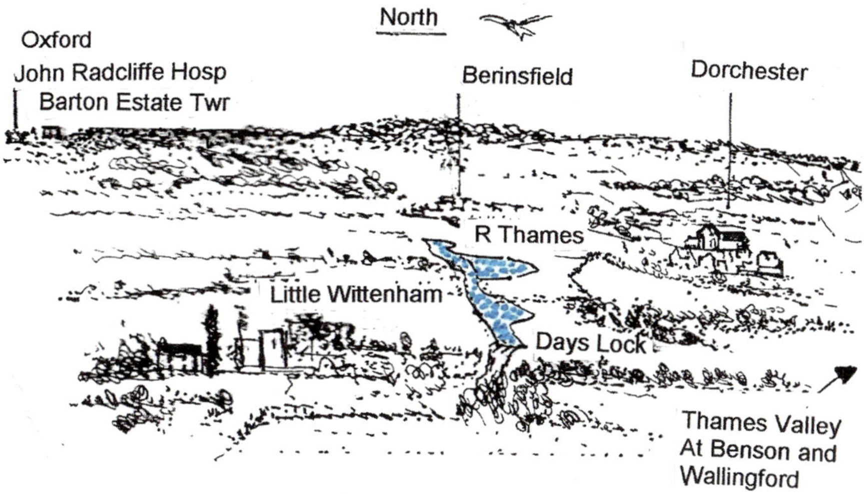

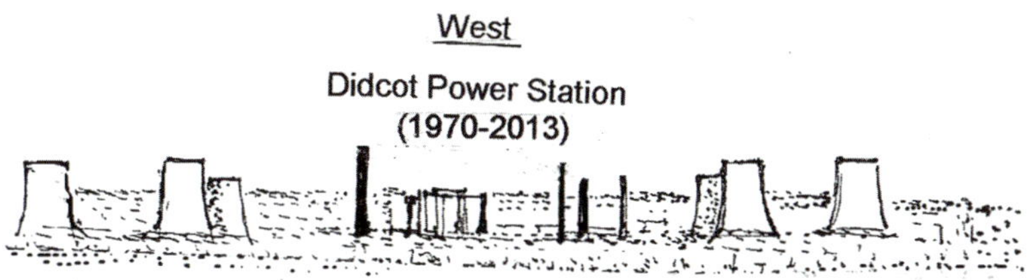

Once out of the woods the path leads to Little Wittenham. It is worth a detour to walk up to Castle Hill and Wittenham Clumps, the trees on top of Round Hill. (Allow one hour or more). Passing through the gate, the isolated church of St. Peter stands where a larger settlement once existed. Members of a family called Dunche are buried here. The tomb and figures, in Tudor dress, of William and his wife, an aunt of Oliver Cromwell, are dated 1594 and 1611. The inscription is in Latin. A plaque reads: Here lyeth buryed William Dunche auditor of the myntes of our late Soveraigne Lordes Kinge Henry the eight and Kinge Edwarde the sixt. Another, Mary, was laid to rest here in 1646.

Little Wittenham.
Below: The Dyke Hills near Dorchester

Facing the church, go right and around to the left and over the bridge. From this side, you can continue to Oxford along the Thames Path passing Clifton Hampden and Abingdon which is very picturesque and Abingdon is full of interest. But that way is six miles further than the following route given:

Here, near Days Lock, head towards the Dyke Hills and Dorchester–upon- Thames. These man made hills are remarkable and date from the Iron Age (around 500 BC). and were used as a fortification. Walk between the mounds, right and up around left along the stony Wittenham Lane in Dorchester. Turn right, then left at St Birinus Catholic church, walking up the High Street past the old coaching inns.

Dorchester-on-Thames

MAP

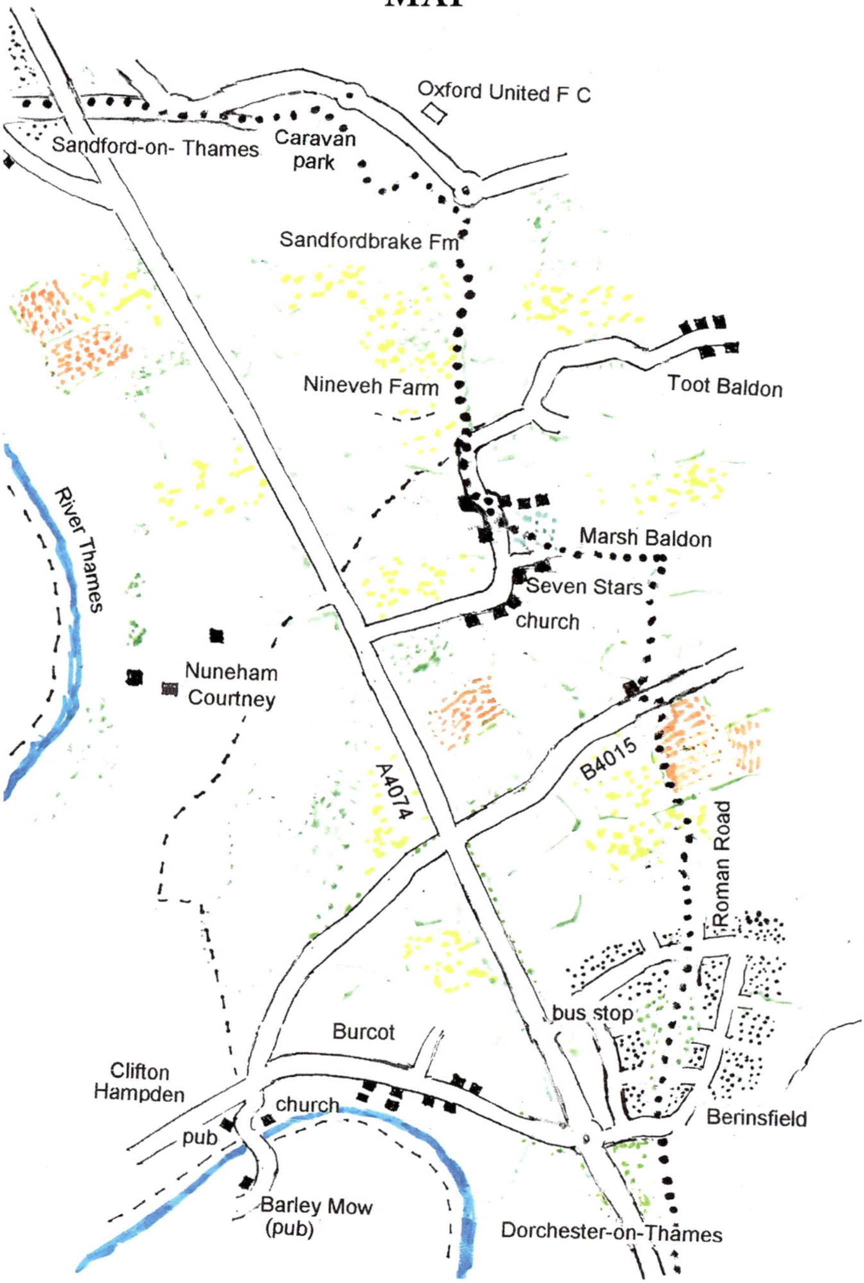
Oxford United F C
Sandford-on- Thames
Caravan park
Sandfordbrake Fm
Nineveh Farm
Toot Baldon
River Thames
Marsh Baldon
Seven Stars
church
Nuneham Courtney
A4074
B4015
Roman Road
bus stop
Burcot
Clifton Hampden
church
pub
Berinsfield
Barley Mow (pub)
Dorchester-on-Thames

DORCHESTER TO SANDFORD-ON-THAMES

The Abbey Church at Dorchester

Dorchester-on-Thames was once a major Roman town and a Saxon one too. In 634 Pope Honorius sent Bishop Birinus here to convert the Saxons to Christianity. A Diocese and Bishopric were established. The Augustinian Abbey was founded in 1140 during Norman times, but was dissolved in 1536 during the rule of Henry V111. The Abbey Church of St Peter and St Paul was rebuilt in the Gothic style. Walk on up to the war memorial, which records 14 casualties of the Great War and 9 from the 1939-45 conflict.

Turn right along Martins Lane, then left and right along the path that crosses the footbridge over the A4074 road. On the far side, go down left, to the path between trees and beside the busy road.

At the George Hotel and (below) the path approaching the footbridge crossing the A4074

This path leads us along to Berinsfield, a modern estate built in the 1960s. The Roman Road from Dorchester to Alchester passes through the middle, where the green space and sports fields are found. Go straight ahead. The old airfield to the east, is where United States Air Forse personnel landed. Bob Hope and Dorothy Lamour came here on their way to entertaining the troops. Glen Miller, the band leader, took his last flight from here, before his plane was lost over the Channel.

Now walk through Evenlode Drive and over to Roman Road, which begins as a concrete lane and soon after, a stony flint track which gives an impression of how the road would have been in Roman times. At the hedge, turn right and soon after go through the gap in the hedge and proceed along a good path to the road.

Along the path to Berinsfield

Walking through Berinsfield

Cautiously cross this road, keeping left to the path opposite, next to the house. Proceed along here with the hedge to the left. This will lead us through Ashen Copse to the lane at the end. Turn left and walk onto the large green at Marsh Baldon. Old houses, thatched cottages and the Seven Stars pub line the left side. Almost out of view is the 12th century St Peters Church, with its curious modified tower. Nearby, the Manor was once owned by a Saxon, but it was given to a Norman noble called Miles Crispin. Baldon House, 17th century, is a listed building.

From the green, walk around the path, right side, to the road. Turn right and walk around the bends, (ignoring the bridle path going left to Clifton Hampden) and at the next corner, go straight on, along the path, with the hedge, right. As the path goes along, below the power lines and then down and over a little bridge, the football stadium of Oxford United comes into view.

Top: The Roman Road.
Below: Marsh Baldon

On the path nearing Oxford

The footpath soon comes out at Grenoble Road. We are now in the City of Oxford, but there are just over 3 miles to go to the finish. Turn left at the roundabout and keep left onto the path with old metal fence posts. Continue along following sharp bends right and left. Pass the caravan and static home park, then onto the road. Cross, then go down left and under the A423 road. Turn right at Henley Road, opposite the Catherine Wheel, cross and now go left into Church Lane.

The old Sandford church was restored at one time and the inscription reads:

Thankes to thy charitie religiofe Dame
Wch found mee old & made mee new again. 1652.

Follow this road around and down to The Kings Arms pub where refreshments may be obtained. Cross the car park and go left to cross Sandford Lock to join the Thames Path, right, all the way into Oxford, two and a half miles distant.

The Catherine Wheel pub and the church, Sandford

MAP

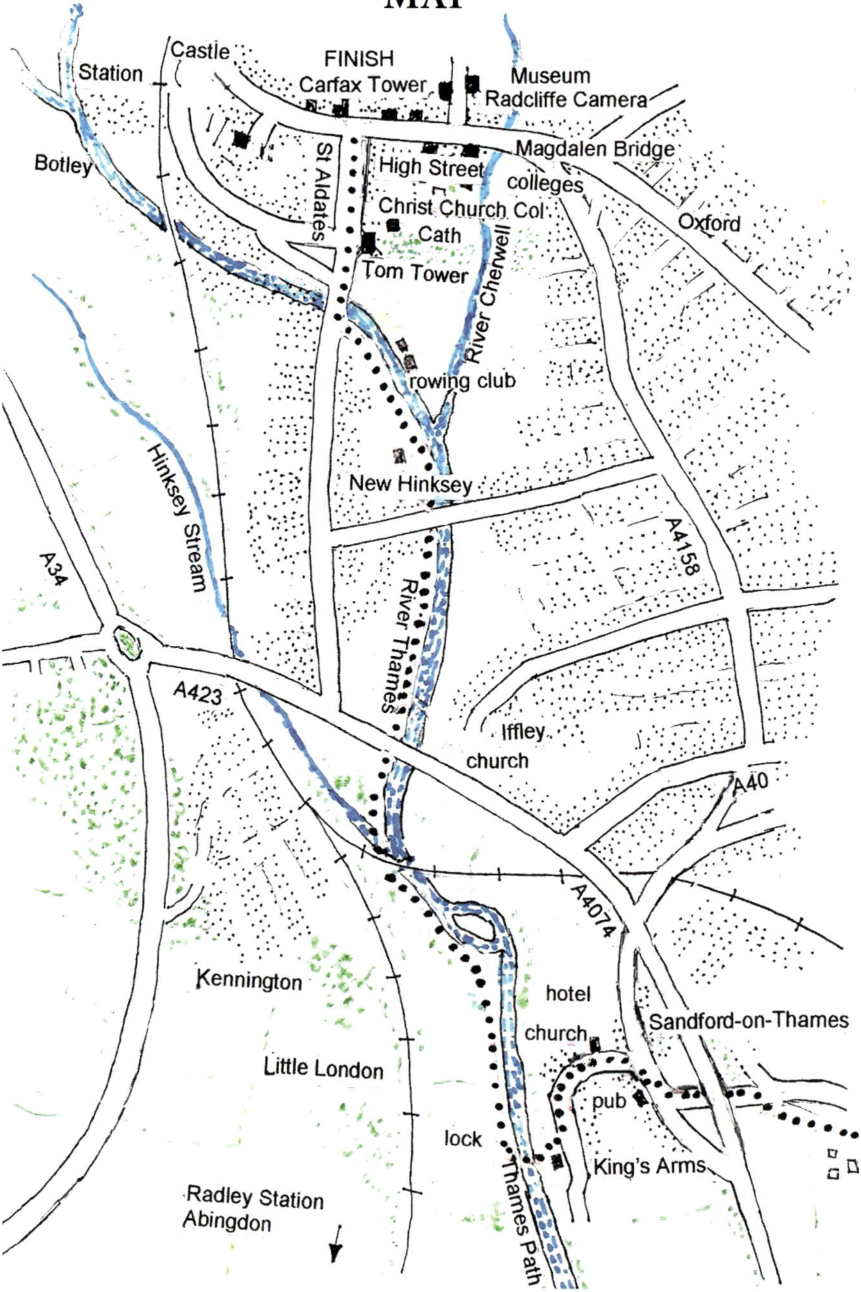
Castle
Station
FINISH
Carfax Tower
Museum
Radcliffe Camera
Botley
St Aldates
High Street
Magdalen Bridge
colleges
Christ Church Col
Cath
Oxford
Tom Tower
River Cherwell
rowing club
Hinksey Stream
New Hinksey
A4158
A34
River Thames
A423
Iffley
church
A40
A4074
Kennington
hotel
church
Sandford-on-Thames
Little London
pub
lock
King's Arms
Thames Path
Radley Station
Abingdon

SANDFORD-ON-THAMES TO OXFORD

The Kings Arms

A notice at the Sandford Lock Keeper's hut tells us that the Romans first used mills, but they didn't come into common use until Saxon times (after 700 AD). At the time of the Domesday Survey in 1086, there were over 5,000 mills recorded. At Sandford Mill, in the 1200s, the Knights Templar used the mill, with its water wheel, for grinding corn. Later it was used for paper making.

Crossing a weir and wooden bridge, then under a railway line and the A423 you soon reach Iffley Lock. This picturesque scene includes weeping willows, old cottages, a church tower and an old stone bridge. Iffley church is one of the finest examples of a Norman church, dating from 1170, with original features.

At Iffley Meadow, are various species of birds - snipe, reed bunting and warblers. Fritillary flowers are also found here. As you near Oxford be aware of cyclists who also use the narrow path! The Isis Farmhouse is often busy, it sells drinks, food and snacks. We are now one mile from the centre of Oxford.

A footbridge nearing Oxford and The Thames at Iffley.

The boat houses of the rowing club are visible across the river as we approach Folly Bridge. The Head of the River pub is another very popular venue for people to relax and socialise. The road leading up right, is St. Aldates and was once known as Great Jewry until 1300. It had Jewish houses and a synagogue. A shop opposite is called Lewis Carroll's Alice Shop. Lewis Carroll was a graduate at Christ Church College and befriended Alice Liddell who became the inspiration for "Alice In Wonderland".

A pleasure boat passing the rowing club. Below: The Head of the River

Christ Church Gardens and Tom Tower, St Aldates

Attractive gardens and Christ Church meadow are passed on the right. Soon you reach Tom Tower, designed by Wren and built in 1681. Great Tom, the bell, weighs 6.3 tons. Looking through the arch and gateway you can see the chapel, also known as Oxford, or Christ Church Cathedral. Christ Church College is the largest in Oxford and was established by Cardinal Wolsley in 1525. The dining hall has also featured as Hogwarts Hall in the Harry Potter films.

As we approach the High Street the next major building on the right is the Town Hall, built in 1895. The Museum of Oxford is here too. Carfax Tower, from which there are splendid views of the dreaming spires of Oxford, is all that remains of the 14th century church of St. Martin, which was demolished in 1896. King Charles II was proclaimed King here in 1660. The word Carfax or *quatre voies* means "four ways", as this was an important crossing place of two major routes. It is interesting to watch the clock strike the quarter hours.

Christ Church College Dining Hall and the Cathedral

The Town Hall

Oxford was first recorded as a place in a Saxon chronicle of 915, but it was in existence long before then. Some claim that the University College was established as a place of learning in the ninth century by Alfred the Great. The oldest college is Merton College (1264). All Souls College, founded by Henry VI in 1483 and Magdalen College are also typically beautiful old buildings of note.

The London to Oxford walk is now completed. There are many sights and places to explore in Oxford. The Ashmolean Museum is the oldest museum in the land and dates from 1683. the Sheldonian Theatre (1669), the Radcliffe Camera and Bodleian Library are worth a visit. At Hertford College is the "Bridge of Sighs". Along the High Street are St. Mary the Virgin Church, the Botanical Gardens and Magdalen Bridge, which crosses the River Cherwell.

The Turf Tavern, a remarkable old pub, is located in Bath Place, a narrow lane under the old City Wall near the Sheldonian Theatre. It was frequented by J R R Tolkien and featured in television's crime drama 'Inspector Morse'.

Above: Carfax Tower and clock detail showing the QuarterBoys and below, looking along the High Street towards Lincoln College

OTHER ROUTES

There are other ways to go between London and Oxford. From Hyde Park Corner, enter Hyde Park and pass the Serpentine Lake (on your right), the Long Water, the Peter Pan statue and the Italian Gardens. This leads to Lancaster Gate. Cross Bayswater Road and proceed along Lancaster Terrace and Sussex Gardens. Turn left along Spring Street and head for Paddington Station. Cross Praed Street and go along Eastbourne Terrace next to the railway station. At the end, turn right and cross the railway bridge which leads to the canal basin of the Grand Union Canal near Little Venice, to the left. Now follow the canal tow path to Bulls Bridge, to join our path after some 12 miles.

At Hammersmith Bridge it is also possible to cross and follow the Thames Path south side, to Kew Bridge. From there, you can cross back again, or follow the riverside path to Richmond and Windsor, all the way to Cookham. You can also follow the Thames Path from Henley to Reading, Goring and Wallingford. These ways are much longer. At Days Lock, near Wallingford, following the Thames Path is enjoyable, as the scenery is very fine and Clifton Hampden and Abingdon (shown right), are very interesting places. This way is about 6 miles longer, but check your maps.

Note: Various parts of the Thames Path will be covered in other routes.

Clifton Hampden church. Below: The bridge, Abingdon
